Arranging For The Small Jazz Ensemble

Arranging For The Small Jazz Ensemble

A Step-by-Step Guide with Practical Exercises and Recorded Examples

Robert Larson

Published by Armfield Academic Press

Editorial Consultants: Bryan Kidd, Graham Breedlove, Steve Fidyk, Craig Fraedrich, Joseph Henson, Matt Niess, Kenny Rittenhouse, Jim Roberts, Regan Brough, Tony Nalker

ISBN: 978-0-9795051-4-0

Library of Congress Control Number: 2010907907

✪

*To my many musician friends, whose advice and great
playing continue to inspire me. . .*

*To my students, who have allowed me the opportunity
to develop the materials that fill these pages. . .*

*And to Karen, Rachel, and Sarah, who tolerated the
long hours of writing, composing, and editing. . .*

I give my heartfelt thanks

Contents

Preface   xi

How to Use This Book   xiii

Part I: Form & Texture   1

1   COMMON SONG FORMS   5

   A Closer Look At Song Forms 5
   Chapter Summary 7

2   THE EXAMPLE TUNES   11

   Swing Example Tune: "Why Not Now" 12
   Latin Example Tune: "Sabrosa" 15
   Ballad Example Piece: "December Serenade" 20
   Chapter Summary 23

3   BASIC ARRANGING STRUCTURES   27

   Instrumental Textures 28
   Basic Arranging Structures 29
   Chapter Summary 33

Part II: The Instruments of the Small Group   39

4   BRASS AND SAXOPHONES   43

   Writing For Wind Instruments 43
   The Trumpet 45
   The Trombone 47
   The Saxophone 49
   Chapter Summary 52

5   The Rhythm Section   57

    Role in the Ensemble   57
    Notating Rhythm Section Parts   58
    The Instruments of the Rhythm Section   60
    Drum Notation   62
    Reinforcement and Integration   63
    Don't Be Intimidated by the Rhythm Section!   64
    Chapter Summary   64

Part III: Jazz Harmony & Voicings   71

6   Tertian Harmony   75

    Close and Open Voicings   76
    Inversions and Positions   79
    The Value of the Piano for Arranging Students   81
    Circle of Fifths Progressions 103
    Choosing a Chord Position   107
    Open Voicings 115
    Chapter Summary   117

7   Quartal Harmony   125

    Quartal Harmony = Drop-2/4   126
    Transposing Quartal Voicings   127
    Quartal Voicings as Four-Note Structures   127
    Quartal Voicings as Dominants   128
    "So What" Voicings   129
    Transposing "So What" Voicings   130
    "So What" and Quartal Voicings in Context   130
    Chapter Summary   131

8   Slash Chords   137

    Uses of Slash Chords   138
    Chord Over Chord   139
    Voicing Summary   142
    Chapter Summary   142

9   Nonharmonic Tones   147

    What is a Nonharmonic Tone in a Jazz Context?   148
    Texture 149
    Approach Techniques   149
    Approach Techniques in Context   154
    Chapter Summary   159

Part IV: Writing An Arrangement   **183**

10 Planning An Arrangement   **187**

Preliminary Steps: Listening and Analysis 187
Brainstorming 188
Transferring Words Into Notation: Three Steps from Sketch to Finished Score 191
Chapter Summary 193

11 Two-Part Writing   **197**

Instrumentation 198
Two-Horn Writing 202
Characteristics of Specific Intervals in Harmony Parts 204
Example Tunes Harmonized in Two Voices 219
Conclusion 245
Chapter Summary 245

12 Four-Part Writing   **249**

Example Pieces Harmonized in Four Voices 251
Conclusion 278
Chapter Summary 278

13 Three-Part Writing   **281**

Three-Part Voicing Structures 281
Example Tunes Voiced in Three Parts 284
Conclusion 286
Chapter Summary 286

14 Introductions   **289**

Common Introduction Types 290
Improvised Introductions 291
Last Section of Melody 292
Vamp 295
Melodic Fragment 298
Unrelated Material 299
Conclusion 303
Chapter Summary 303

15 Endings   **307**

Stock Endings 308
Common Ending Types 309
Tags 309
Vamp 315
Melodic Fragment 317
Unrelated Material: Vamp 318
Unrelated Material: Newly Composed Section 320
Chapter Summary 322

16 COMMON PROBLEMS & SOLUTIONS   **325**

Parallel Harmonies 329
Awkward Lines 333
Awkward Repeated Notes 335
Overwriting 337
Lack of Integration with the Rhythm Section 339
The "Correct" Version 341
Chapter Summary 343

17 THE COMPLETE ARRANGEMENT   **345**

Creating the Score and Parts 346
"Why Not Now" 348
"Sabrosa" 366
"December Serenade" 385
"Finding the Groove" 392
Chapter Summary 402

18 CONCLUSION   **405**

Appendices   **407**

A TUNES FOR EXERCISES   **409**

ABAC Swing Exercise Tune 410
AABA Latin Exercise Tune 412
AABA Ballad Exercise Tune 414

B SAMPLE PART   **417**

C STAFF PAPER   **421**

Plain staff paper for general use 423
Three-staff sketch paper (portrait orientation) 425
Three-staff sketch paper (landscape orientation) 427
Score paper for two horns and rhythm 429
Score paper for three horns and rhythm 431
Score paper for four horns and rhythm 433

INDEX   **435**

Preface

In order to survive in today's music world, one must wear many hats—that of player, teacher, businessman, and a host of others. But for the jazz musician, the importance of having good arranging skills cannot be overstated. Improvisation, composition, and arranging are at times so intertwined that they become almost indistinguishable from one another. Therefore, every student of jazz needs to have at least some arranging chops.

Like many musicians, I was a player before I was an arranger. While I enjoyed writing music early in my career, I was unsure of how best to express my intentions to other musicians. I recall feeling comfortable writing for rhythm section instruments (since I am a pianist) but intimidated when I needed to add horns into the mix. Through trial and error, I found that transferring my knowledge of elements such as voicings, style, and form from the piano keyboard to the small group or big band score was not as difficult as I had feared. Studying with successful arrangers further confirmed that I was on the right track. Thus began my journey of organizing in my own mind a step-by-step method which enabled me make the leap from player to arranger.

The materials presented in this book are the product not only of my experiences as an arranger, but from over twenty years of teaching jazz arranging courses at the college level. I have used this method to help many students write successful arrangements, and I sincerely hope that you will find it useful as well. Regardless of where your musical career takes you, any time you spend studying arranging will offer a valuable return on your investment.

Robert Larson

How to Use This Book

This book may be used as the textbook for the first unit of a jazz arranging sequence at a college or university or by a self-taught individual for personal study. It was designed with several built-in features to make it well-organized, user-friendly, and above all, educational. The following tips have been provided to help you obtain the maximum benefit from the book.

Use the Website

Supporting materials for this book are located at www.SmallJazzEnsemble.com, which is the book's website. All of the audio examples, the assignments in PDF format, transposed scores, staff and score paper, and short instructional videos pertaining to various jazz arranging topics are located here.

Before You Get Started

If you are reading this right now, you are probably already a jazz lover. But in addition to a love of jazz, you should also have some background in jazz theory. Aspiring arrangers should have (in addition to a good sense of jazz style) a basic familiarity with chords, scales, and lead sheets.

Example Tunes

I composed three example tunes especially for this book. These tunes appear throughout the book in various incarnations—they are first introduced in chapter 2, then used throughout the book to demonstrate various techniques and concepts, and finally presented as complete small group arrangements in chapter 17. An additional tune is used to illustrate common arranging errors.

Audio Recordings

There are audio recordings of many of the musical examples in this book. All of these recordings are offered free of charge at www.SmallJazzEnsemble.com. Be on the lookout for this symbol:

Whenever you see that symbol next to a musical example, be sure to listen to the recording with the corresponding track number.

Assignments

Throughout the book you will find various assignments that parallel the exercises that I give my own arranging students. At first, these assignments are very specific and detailed, covering such topics as instrumentation, voicings, countermelodies, etc. Later in the book, however, the assignments build upon the fundamental skills learned earlier as the student begins to create actual arrangements. I have composed three original tunes, found in appendix A, that will be used as the basis for the arrangements assigned to the reader.

Some of you will be using this book for personal study, while others will be using it as the textbook for an arranging class. Therefore, I have provided several options for completing the assignments. Choose the method that is most appropriate for you.

- Download an assignment in PDF format from the book's website. Print it out. Write on that page. Turn it in to your teacher (if required).
- Photocopy an assignment from the book. Write on the photocopy. Turn it in to your teacher (if required).
- *Carefully* tear out an assignment from this book. Write on that page. Turn it in to your teacher if required. The reverse page of each assignment has been left blank.

Free Staff Paper

In the back of the book (in appendix C) I have provided several useful varieties of staff paper that you may photocopy freely. There are blank staff paper templates for general use, sketching, and scoring for small group. These staff paper templates are also provided as PDF documents on the website for your convenience.

Get Your Music Played

The goal of this book is to teach you how to write for a small jazz ensemble. For a budding arranger, however, the most educational experience you can have does not come from a book but rather from actual playing situations. Hearing your music played by real musicians is the most valuable learning laboratory there is because the players will give you valuable feedback on what you have written. After all the hard work of planning, sketching, and writing the chart, don't neglect to have your charts played by a real band. The first time you hear your own music performed is sure to be a thrilling experience.

Part I

Form & Texture

What goes into the creation of a great jazz arrangement? Are there arrangers who just start writing and it comes out swingin'? Undoubtedly there are those who have the gift to hear in their minds how an arrangement should go and they then just write it out. If Mozart were a jazz musician, I'm sure he'd be one of these lucky few. For the rest of us, however, it's a different story. Most successful jazz arrangements are constructed through plenty of hard work and careful deliberation. They normally don't just happen by chance.

Before a chef prepares a meal, he or she must first understand how each ingredient tastes and how they blend together. Likewise, a musician must also grasp the parts in order to create the whole. A chef uses his or her taste buds to evaluate and learn about the characteristics of each ingredient and the craft of cooking; musicians use their ears by practicing careful listening.

In each of the first three chapters of this book, the reader is encouraged to listen and to become aware of the flow and direction of jazz tunes. Song form is explored in chapter 1. Chapter 2 introduces the tunes used throughout this book for study. Chapter 3 begins the exploration of texture and jazz arranging form.

Common Song Forms

An important early step to becoming a jazz arranger is to gain an understanding of the different types of song forms that are common in the jazz tradition. In music, form involves the organization of elements such as time, melody, and harmony into relationships. There are actually only a few forms that dominate the jazz repertoire. Understanding these simple forms (and they are indeed simple compared to their classical counterparts) can help a novice arranger organize the melodic and harmonic materials in ways that work consistently.

The four tunes composed especially for this book follow these basic forms. Also, these tunes represent the most common styles found in jazz: swing and Latin. The tempos vary from ballad tempo to medium-up. In this book the term *tune* is synonymous with the classical term *piece*. *Piece* is just too formal a word for a book about jazz!

A Closer Look At Song Forms

As I mentioned a moment ago, jazz standards tend to follow one of several common song forms. The most common forms for a jazz standard are AABA, ABAC and the

The Origins of Jazz Standards

Many of today's best-known jazz standards were never intended to become the enduring, iconic compositions we know today. A large number of these songs started out as show tunes (i.e., part of some kind of stage musical), many from Tin Pan Alley. In the days before the widespread popularity of recorded music, a great number of music publishers had offices in the Tin Pan Alley district of Manhattan. Aspiring composers would flock to these publishing houses hoping to sell their songs and make a quick buck. Other times, staff writers would supply new songs for these publishers. These companies would then make a profit by selling the songs in the form of sheet music, arranged for piano and voice. When a publishing house found a song that it liked, it would push to get the song used in an upcoming Broadway show. The exposure from these shows would then drive sheet music sales for the publisher. Sometimes a composer's song would appear in a musical revue with the songs of other composers, and other times the entire score for a Broadway show would be written by one composer. All of the composers of today's great jazz standards (such as Irving Berlin, Cole Porter, George Gershwin, Jerome Kern and Richard Rodgers) wrote tunes for Broadway musicals and Hollywood movies.

blues. Since it is so crucial for an arranger to have a thorough understanding of song forms, let's take a moment to examine each of these three song forms individually.

AABA Form

The AABA form is perhaps the most common song form in jazz music. The main theme (usually eight measures long) is stated twice and is followed by a contrasting bridge also eight measures in length. The form concludes with a final restatement of the A section. Some well-known tunes that have an AABA form are "Take the A Train," "Have You Met Miss Jones," "What Is This Thing Called Love," and "Honeysuckle Rose."

Typical arrangements present the entire melodic form (known as the *head*) once before the improvised solos or before any newly composed material such as a shout chorus. At the end of the piece, the entire melody of the song is usually restated. Sometimes, instead of finishing the tune by playing the entire melody, the arrangement returns to the bridge and then concludes with just the bridge and last A section of the tune.

ABAC Form

Another extremely common song form is ABAC form. Although each section is normally eight measures in length, it is useful to think of this form as two sixteen measure sections. In the first half, the main theme (A) leads to an eight measure contrasting section (B). The second sixteen measure section also begins with A, but concludes with a section (C) that provides a contrast with B. Some well-known tunes that have an ABAC form are "In A Mellow Tone," "On Green Dolphin Street," "I Could Write A Book," "I Left My Heart in San Francisco," and "Just Friends."

Similar to the AABA form, a typical arrangement of an ABAC tune will state the entire head once before the improvised solos or other material. At the end of the piece, the entire melody of the song is usually restated. Sometimes instead of finishing the tune by playing the entire melody, the arrangement will return to the second A section and finish by stating only the last A and C sections.

The Twelve-Bar Blues

The twelve-bar blues (usually just called *the blues*) is perhaps the most important song form in jazz and popular music. The origin of the blues is rooted in the "call and response" traditions of African-American folk music. Contemporary treatments of a blues often retain this "call and response" relationship. The blues is probably also the form most familiar to the novice jazz listener. "C Jam Blues," "Tenor Madness," and "Now's the Time" are examples of well-known blues tunes.

In the next chapter we will study these song forms further as we examine the example tunes.

Chapter Summary

1. The most important forms in jazz music are AABA, ABAC and the blues.
2. Arrangers must develop a thorough understanding of these common song forms.

Assignment 1.1

Song Form Analysis

1. Analyze the form of several tunes from a fake book. Determine whether each tune is AABA, ABAC, blues, or some other form.

2. Listen to several jazz recordings. Without looking at a lead sheet, analyze and identify the form of each tune.

The Example Tunes

The purpose of this chapter is to familiarize you with the compositions written especially for this book. Each tune has an accompanying recording which is indicated by the special audio icon at the beginning of each tune. After each lead sheet, a harmonic analysis of the tune is given to stimulate further study. In each harmonic analysis, the chords are rendered only in root position. Of course, these root position chords are unsuitable for actual arranging; they are presented here only for the sake of study and analysis.

Because of the harmonic complexity of some example tunes (such as "Sabrosa" and "December Serenade") several of the chords included in the analysis contain upper extensions. While working through the text, refer back to these analyses so that you keep the harmonic context in mind as you explore the various arranging techniques. The more familiar you are with the example tunes, the more you will get out of the examples and illustrations found in later chapters.

While there are four tunes composed for this book, only three are presented in this chapter. The fourth, a blues, can be found in chapter 16 in which we explore common arranging mistakes.

Swing Example Tune: "Why Not Now"

"Why Not Now," our first example tune, is an up-tempo swing tune with an AABA form. It employs a modified "I Got Rhythm" chord progression (the chord progression of George Gershwin's famous song "I Got Rhythm" often called simply "rhythm changes"). This piece is a challenge to arrange because of the speed and motion of the melody. Choosing the appropriate instrument to play the melody will be particularly important.

WHY NOT NOW

Analysis of "Why Not Now"

"Why Not Now," while similar to the "I Got Rhythm" chord progression in some ways, also contains a unique series of ii–V movements beginning in measure 4. Also, notice the text boxes which identify chord substitutions. The key centers of the bridge move in minor thirds: Gb–A–C.

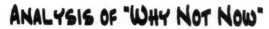

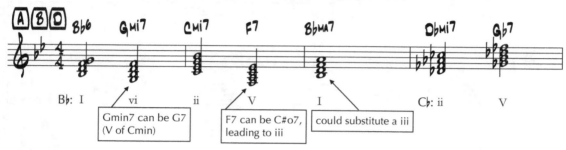

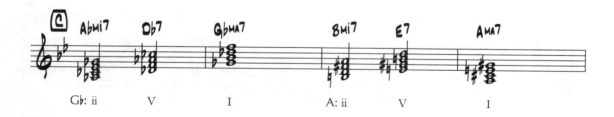

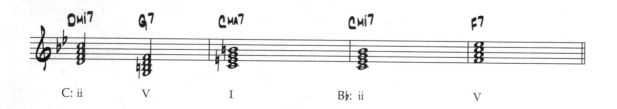

Latin Example Tune: "Sabrosa"

"Sabrosa," our Latin example tune, is a sixty-four bar AABA composition. Each section is sixteen bars long (twice as long as what you would find in most jazz standards). The bridge offers an interesting opportunity for the arranger as it travels to a rather distant key.

Sabrosa

Analysis of "Sabrosa"

As you will see reflected in the analysis on the following page, "Sabrosa" is a complicated tune. But the harmony is functional, and while there is some modal interchange (i.e., borrowed chords) occurring (see measure 4, the III+ of F minor), there are also simple progressions as well. As a result, the voice leading will be relatively smooth.

ANALYSIS OF "SABROSA"

TTS = tritone substitution
PC = passing chord
BC = borrowed chord

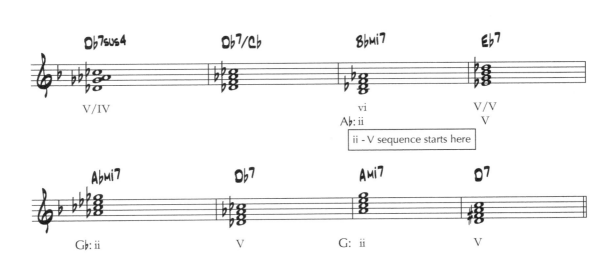

Ballad Example Piece: "December Serenade"

"December Serenade," our ballad example tune, has a modified ABAC form in which the final section is only four measures long. The most attractive feature of this tune is its harmonic color. The opening descending melody includes long tones on rich dominant ♯11 chords. Later, we will discover that measures 2 and 4 are logical places for a countermelody.

Analysis of "December Serenade"

"December Serenade" is comprised primarily of sequential falling fifth movements that shift the key center every two measures. It also features modal interchange in which the V of III (the E7 in measure 12) resolves to the III of F minor. The tune concludes with a bluesy-sounding line that is supported by a dominant chord cycle culminating on a tritone substitution (the Bma7(♭5)) of the tonic chord (F).

ANALYSIS OF "DECEMBER SERENADE"

Chapter Summary

1. Much of this book revolves around the example tunes.
2. The example tunes will be used to teach the nuts and bolts of arranging.
3. Study the example tunes carefully so you benefit fully from what comes later.
4. As you work through the book you will need to refer back to the lead sheets and analyses of the example tunes.

Assignment 2.1

The Example Tunes

Familiarize yourself thoroughly with the example tunes given in this chapter. Listen to the recording of each tune until you can sing the head from memory. Also study the lead sheet of each tune, playing the chords on the piano if possible.

Basic Arranging Structures

Creating an arrangement is similar to building any complex structure. The jazz arranger brings together disparate elements in order to create what is hopefully a unified whole. Since music exists in time, the order of events is critical for an arrangement to make sense to the listener.

Musical form is created by rhythm, melody, harmony, instrumentation, and texture. We have already seen the first three of these elements in the discussion of song forms in chapter 1, as well as in the analyses of the example tunes in chapter 2. Song forms such as AABA, ABAC, and blues may be created using only these three elements; when we add the last two elements (instrumentation and texture) more complex musical creations may result. In chapters 4 and 5 we will discuss issues of instrumentation in detail. Texture, the fifth element, provides one more way in which to build the structure of an arrangement.

Instrumental Textures

The word *texture* is often used to describe how something feels to the touch—the roughness of sandpaper or how ice cream melts in your mouth. Musical texture obviously refers to how something sounds. There can be light musical textures (e.g., flute and harp) or heavy textures (e.g., bass trombone, euphonium, and tuba). What we're talking about here is how instruments are combined and how those combinations affect the structure of the arrangement.

There are only a few ways to combine instruments. In its simplest form, the writing process for two or more horns can be organized into four possible textures:

1. Unisons (or octaves)
2. Homophony
3. Polyphony
4. A combination of two or more of the above

Let's take a moment to examine each of these important textures in a bit more depth.

Unison

Sometimes, when one of my students turns in an arranging project, he or she says something like this: "I couldn't think of anything else to do, so I just wrote unison horn parts." My response: "Bravo!" Simple does not mean inferior. Combining two or more horns in unison or octaves achieves one very important goal: A new instrumental timbre is formed from the combination of two or more instruments. Blending instruments will be discussed in chapter 11. For now, just keep in mind that simply having the horns play the same pitches, either in unison or at the octave, is an effective way to combine instruments.

Homophony

By the late fifteenth century, two textures had come to dominate Western music: homophony and polyphony. Homophony occurs when a melody dominates other voices, and these accompanying voices generally follow the rhythm and contour of the melody. The melody is normally the top voice in this texture. This is a very common texture in all kinds of music—from the saxophone soli to gospel piano playing to the barbershop quartet.

Polyphony

In polyphonic music, the individual parts are independent of one another. The best example of polyphony is the music of J.S. Bach. If you listen to a fugue from *The Well-Tempered Clavier* you will instantly understand what this texture sounds like. To write polyphonically is to view music in a horizontal fashion. A primary difference from homophony is in the realm of rhythm. The individual voices in a polyphonic texture do not normally follow the rhythm of a predominant melody as in homophony.

Greek Roots

The words *homophony* and *polyphony* are based on Greek root words. The word *homophony* comes from two Greek roots: *homos* and *phone* (FO-nay). The word *homos* means "same" and the word *phone* means "sound" or "voice." So literally the word *homophony* means "same sound" or "same voice." The word *polyphony* also comes from Greek roots: *polloi* and *phone*. The Greek word *polloi* means "many." So literally, the word *polyphony* means "many sounds" or "many voices."

A Combination of the Above

Although it is perfectly acceptable to write an arrangement that is dominated by any of the textures described above, arrangers often use a combination of these textures. For example, a homophonic A section could lead to a polyphonic repeated A section which could then lead to a unison or solo bridge. The goal is to make these textures flow logically from one to another. This concept will be discussed at length throughout the remainder of the book.

A Further Simplification

The four textures discussed above may be reduced even further. In fact, the sample charts discussed in this book are arranged for two and four horns using the following two simplified textures:

1. Unison, octave, and/or homophonic texture (hereafter referred to as "homophonic/unison texture")
2. A blend of polyphonic writing with elements of unison, octaves, and homophony (hereafter referred to as "combination texture")

In my experience, these two simplified textures work extremely well, and I have found it useful to consolidate my approach to arranging in this manner. As you listen to the example tunes scored in these two textures, you may have a hard time deciding which version works best. There is no one "correct" way to arrange a tune; our goal is to create an arrangement that has a logical and natural flow.

Basic Arranging Structures

There are many ways to structure an arrangement for small group, but there are certain "stock" road maps that have developed over the years. As a student of jazz arranging, you should strive to become intimately familiar with these very common road maps in the same manner that a student of classical music studies classical forms. As you gain more confidence in your skills, you will probably want to venture away from these stock arrangements. But in the meantime, they will prove very useful for students because these can be relied upon to work *every time*.

The diagrams presented on the next few pages illustrate these stock arrangements. Diagrams are given for AABA, ABAC, and blues song forms. As you study them, pay particular attention to the flow and direction represented by the arrows. Notice that in each case the arrangement develops as the result of changes in instrumental texture. However, there is also a certain amount of unity within each individual diagram. For example, in the AABA 32-measure song form illustrated below, the unison scoring suggested for the first A section is thickened in the second A section by harmony or by the presence of a countermelody. However, scoring the last A section in the same fashion as the second A section serves to unify the arrangement. Each type of stock arrangement illustrated in these diagrams demonstrates a balance of continuity and development.

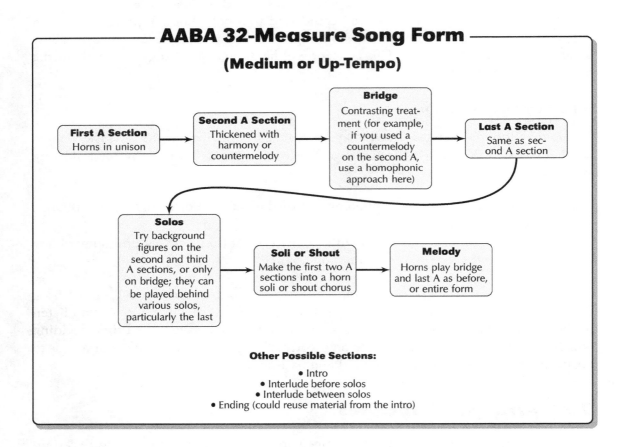

AABA 32-Measure Song Form

(Medium or Up-Tempo)

First A Section
Horns in unison

Second A Section
Thickened with harmony or countermelody

Bridge
Contrasting treatment (for example, if you used a countermelody on the second A, use a homophonic approach here)

Last A Section
Same as second A section

Solos
Try background figures on the second and third A sections, or only on bridge; they can be played behind various solos, particularly the last

Soli or Shout
Make the first two A sections into a horn soli or shout chorus

Melody
Horns play bridge and last A as before, or entire form

Other Possible Sections:
• Intro
• Interlude before solos
• Interlude between solos
• Ending (could reuse material from the intro)

ABAC 32-Measure Song Form

(Medium or Up-Tempo)

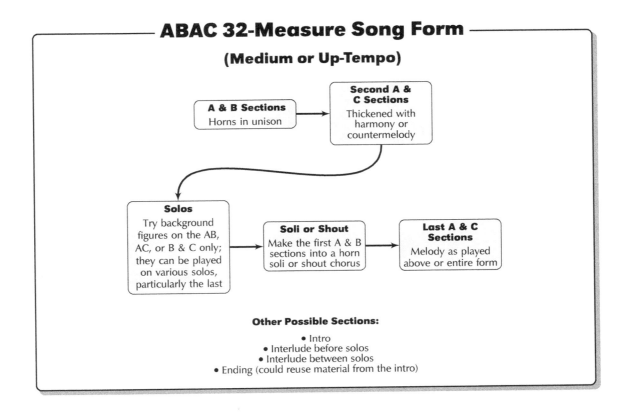

A & B Sections
Horns in unison

Second A & C Sections
Thickened with harmony or countermelody

Solos
Try background figures on the AB, AC, or B & C only; they can be played on various solos, particularly the last

Soli or Shout
Make the first A & B sections into a horn soli or shout chorus

Last A & C Sections
Melody as played above or entire form

Other Possible Sections:
- Intro
- Interlude before solos
- Interlude between solos
- Ending (could reuse material from the intro)

AABA 32-Measure Song Form

(Ballad Tempo)

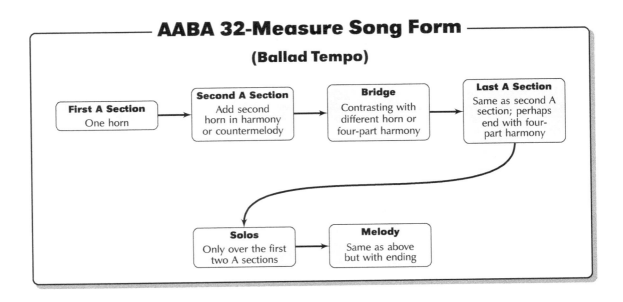

First A Section
One horn

Second A Section
Add second horn in harmony or countermelody

Bridge
Contrasting with different horn or four-part harmony

Last A Section
Same as second A section; perhaps end with four-part harmony

Solos
Only over the first two A sections

Melody
Same as above but with ending

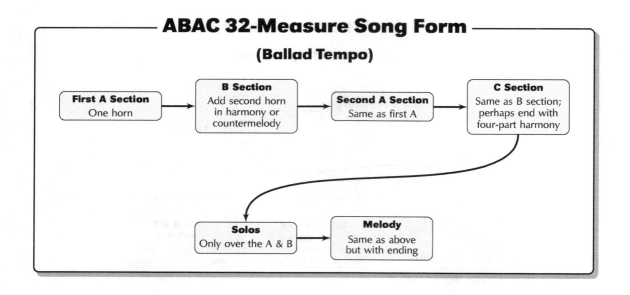

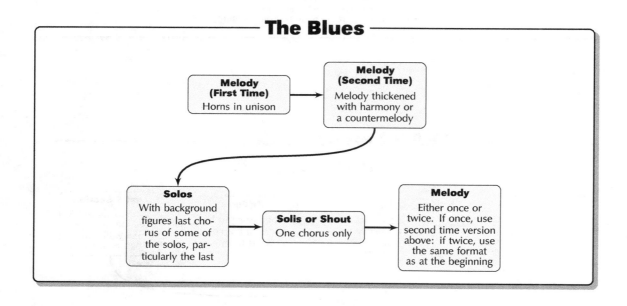

The diagrams on the previous pages are obviously not the only way to expand these song forms into full arrangements. I urge you to try them, however, so that your first arrangements have an excellent chance of succeeding in terms of form.

We will revisit the discussion of texture as we proceed through the book. A slight detour is needed at this point as we explore the instruments of the small jazz ensemble.

Chapter Summary

1. Musical form is created by rhythm, melody, harmony, instrumentation, and texture.

2. A homophonic texture occurs when a melody dominates the other voices, and they all move together.

3. A polyphonic texture occurs when individual parts are independent of one another.

4. Textures can be simplified into the following:

   (a) Homophonic/unison
   (b) Combination of unison, homophonic, and polyphonic

5. There are stock arrangements of the basic forms of AABA, ABAC, and blues that arrangers have developed.

Assignment 3.1

Schematic Diagrams

Locate several recordings of two-horn, three-horn, or four-horn arrangements. On a separate sheet of paper, make schematic diagrams of them. Choose tunes that represent the various song forms (i.e., AABA, ABAC, blues). Below is a list of suggested artists whose small group recordings would be well-suited for this assignment.

- Horace Silver
- Art Blakey
- Benny Golson
- Tom Harrell
- Woody Shaw
- Joe Henderson
- Lee Morgan
- Clifford Brown/Max Roach

In your schematic diagram, indicate the following elements:

- General information about the tune
- Instrumentation (e.g., *tutti*, in which all the horns are scored together; *solo*, in which one horn is featured; *duet*, for two horns, etc.)
- Rhythmic feel (e.g., in two, in four, rubato)
- General comments about instrumental texture
- Role of the rhythm section (level of integration with horn parts)
- Other items of interest

To help you complete this assignment, examine the example on the next page.

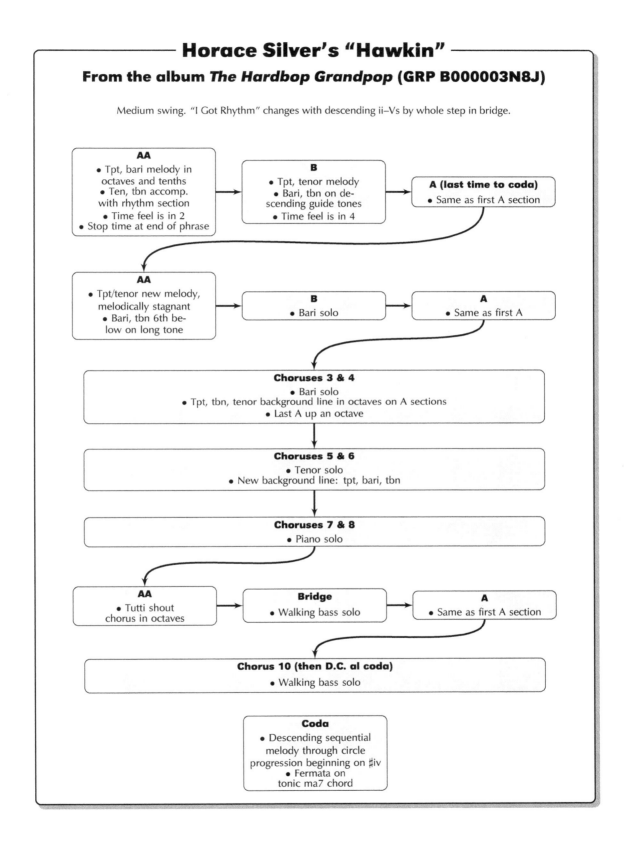

Horace Silver's "Hawkin"

From the album *The Hardbop Grandpop* (GRP B000003N8J)

Medium swing. "I Got Rhythm" changes with descending ii–Vs by whole step in bridge.

AA
- Tpt, bari melody in octaves and tenths
- Ten, tbn accomp. with rhythm section
- Time feel is in 2
- Stop time at end of phrase

B
- Tpt, tenor melody
- Bari, tbn on descending guide tones
- Time feel is in 4

A (last time to coda)
- Same as first A section

AA
- Tpt/tenor new melody, melodically stagnant
- Bari, tbn 6th below on long tone

B
- Bari solo

A
- Same as first A

Choruses 3 & 4
- Bari solo
- Tpt, tbn, tenor background line in octaves on A sections
- Last A up an octave

Choruses 5 & 6
- Tenor solo
- New background line: tpt, bari, tbn

Choruses 7 & 8
- Piano solo

AA
- Tutti shout chorus in octaves

Bridge
- Walking bass solo

A
- Same as first A section

Chorus 10 (then D.C. al coda)
- Walking bass solo

Coda
- Descending sequential melody through circle progression beginning on ♯iv
- Fermata on tonic ma7 chord

Part II

The Instruments of the Small Group

Small instrumental jazz ensembles are typically comprised of several horn players plus a rhythm section. Part II will explore the instruments typically found in small jazz groups.

It is important to understand the construction and sonic characteristics of the instruments you are writing for. Also, understanding how each instrument functions and behaves in various parts of the range is a must for arrangers. In chapter 4, we will explore the characteristics of the trumpet, the trombone and the saxophone focusing on their range, timbre, and transposition. These wind instruments are by far the most frequently used in jazz.

Chapter 5 is devoted to the rhythm section. This special section is one of the important ways that jazz ensembles differ from other musical organizations. The presence of a section whose primary function is to supply the rhythmic and harmonic framework is reminiscent of music written hundreds of years ago during the Baroque period, when harpsichordists and cellists fulfilled the roles now held by pianists, bassists, guitarists, and drummers.

The more you know about the instruments for which you are writing the better—so try to learn as much as you can about them. It is useful for arrangers and composers to have at least some experience actually playing these instruments even if at a very basic level.

Brass and Saxophones

Since I am a pianist, writing for wind instruments was at first somewhat intimidating to me. But my comfort level increased considerably once I understood how each of the wind instruments functions. Listening was also a crucial learning tool—as I listened to many recordings and performances which featured wind instruments, I began to develop an understanding of the way these instruments are used in jazz. I also had many conversations with other musicians I knew who played these instruments and they gave me invaluable advice about writing for their instruments.

The information in this chapter will help you understand the characteristics of the trumpet, the trombone, and the saxophone family. In addition to reading about these instruments, you should also do plenty of listening—and don't forget to ask for advice from those who play these instruments.

Writing For Wind Instruments

When writing for wind instruments, the arranger must keep in mind several important issues: the range of the instrument, the tessitura the instrument will be playing in, how that instrument will perform when combined with other instruments, and the articulations you want for each note played.

Memorize the Ranges

It is critical that the arranger memorize the ranges of all the instruments. Obviously, you must not write notes in your arrangements that your musicians won't be able to play. This is annoying to musicians and makes you look incompetent as an arranger.

Range and Region Considerations

Some notes speak better than others on the various instruments. If you write in the transposed staff (especially in the top half of it) all of the instruments will function beautifully. When you start to use ledger lines, be careful! Perhaps another instrument would be more comfortable playing what you have in mind. There will be times when placing an instrument in an uncharacteristic situation (a baritone saxophone in the upper register, for instance) will result in a beautiful and unexpected timbre. As you gain more experience, you may want to experiment in this manner—but for now, be conservative with your range choices.

Instrument Combinations and Blend

The tone quality of any given instrument depends on several factors. First, the material that the instrument is made of will have a big influence over how it sounds. Also, the shape of the bore (e.g., conical, cylindrical, or a mix of both) will affect the brightness or mellowness of the tone. Overtones are important—the presence or absence of overtones in a sound give a certain tone much of its uniqueness. And finally, the method of tone production (e.g., the buzzing of the lips, the plucking of a string, the vibrations of a cane reed) gives a tone much of its distinct sound. These factors are used to divide musical instruments into families such as the woodwind family, brass family, string family, and percussion family.

As you think about combining instruments, be aware that you are creating a new sound by blending the tone qualities of each individual instrument. Scoring within an instrument family will create the most homogeneous sound. Combining instruments from different families but with a similar timbre and range (e.g., trombone and tenor sax) blend well but result in a more diverse tone color than two instruments from the same family. Combining instruments from different families with different timbre and range (e.g., flute and trombone) can create very unique and exotic sounds.

By this time in the history of jazz, just about every instrument combination has been tried, but there are some that work better than others. For instance, if you choose a very standard instrumentation (e.g., trumpet, alto sax, tenor sax, and trombone) it is sure to work. This advice is not intended to stifle your creativity as you begin to write your own arrangements, but to encourage you to build upon the experiments of the great jazz composers and arrangers who have come before you. As you gain more experience, you might want to write for more unique combinations of instruments. For now, however, enjoy the success you are sure to have by using a tried-and-true instrument combination.

Articulation Markings

Although experienced jazz musicians are well-trained as jazz stylists, the arranger must include articulation markings on notes that could be interpreted in several ways. While all of the aspects of jazz style are beyond the scope of this book, you should be aware of the following articulation markings, and use them to convey exactly what you want to hear from the horn players and also the rhythm section players. Here are the four most commonly used articulation markings used in jazz notation:

Example 4.1

The first symbol, which indicates a short note, is called a *staccato*. The second marking, which indicates that a note should be held for its full value, is called a *long mark*. The classical term for this mark is *tenuto*. The third symbol is called an *accent*. It means that the note associated with it should be given extra emphasis. This marking is sometimes referred to as a *regular accent* or perhaps even a *sideways accent* to distinguish it from the fourth symbol, which points upward. This symbol, called a *rooftop accent*, indicates that the note associated with it should be short, yet accented. The classical term for this mark is *marcato*.

The Trumpet

Trumpet players were among the earliest major innovators in jazz. Buddy Bolden, King Oliver, Louis Armstrong, and Bix Beiderbecke were crucial contributors in the development of jazz as either trumpet or cornet players. The trumpet's importance as a jazz instrument continues to the present day. The lead trumpet player in a big band is largely responsible for setting the style of the entire ensemble. Also, because of the trumpet's power and bright tone, it is a natural choice for the melody in small group writing. The arrangements in this book feature the trumpet prominently, scored as both the primary melodic instrument and in countermelodies.

The trumpet sound is produced by buzzing the lips on a mouthpiece, which causes the air column within the instrument to vibrate. By tightening or loosening the lips, the player can play the various partials of the overtone series. Furthermore, pressing the valves reroutes the air through longer or shorter lengths of tubing, changing the length of the instrument. Therefore, changes in pitch are a result of either moving to a different partial, changing the length of the tubing, or both.

Arrangers must fully understand these physical characteristics of the trumpet because they greatly affect the types of musical lines that are feasible for the player. For instance, arrangers should avoid writing uncomfortable leaps in trumpet parts—a wide leap might require the player to change from one partial to another in an awkward manner.

The most important considerations to keep in mind when writing for trumpet are range and endurance. It is important to keep the music in a range that is comfortable for the player. Also, trumpet players must have opportunities to rest their chops, particularly when playing in the upper register. A common error made by student arrangers is to overwrite the trumpet part, so be sure to avoid writing parts that are too high, too busy, or too difficult.

The trumpet's bright tone comes from the shape of its bore, which is primarily cylindrical. The cornet and flugelhorn, on the other hand, get their more mellow-sounding tones from their primarily conical bore. That's why a trumpet player will sometimes pull out a flugelhorn when called upon to play something lyrical such as a ballad. Thus the contour of the bore affects the tone quality of brass instruments—the same is true with woodwinds.

Trumpet Notation

Music for the trumpet is written in the treble clef. Since the trumpet is pitched in the key of B♭, music written for trumpet must be transposed up a whole step from concert pitch as shown in the following example:

Example 4.2

Of course, key signatures for the B♭ trumpet must also be transposed up one whole step by adding sharps or subtracting flats as shown here.

Example 4.3

Trumpet Range

Arranging students need to memorize instrumental ranges. Understanding how the instrument behaves within its range is also critical, but the arranger must never write notes beyond the range of the instrument.

The following example shows the range of the trumpet. The arrow indicates that the upper range depends upon the player—this will vary, of course, from player to player. It is appropriate, however, to write below the written high D in small group writing. The highest register is typically reserved for a big band setting.

Example 4.4

The Registers of the Trumpet

The low range of the trumpet, including notes below the staff, is difficult to control. Intonation can be inconsistent, and the tone is quite muddy. Avoid writing leaps into this area. As the trumpet range moves into the staff, projection, endurance, and agility all improve significantly. The dynamic range is also increased. The tone becomes brighter and clearer as the trumpet range moves to the top of the staff, but it also becomes more difficult to play softly in this area. The range above the staff is a powerful part of the trumpet range. Remember that endurance can be a real challenge in this register—even accomplished players need occasional rests if they are asked to play in this range for extended periods.

Trumpet Mutes

Although only two brass instruments are explored in this book (trumpet and trombone) they can both be fitted with mutes that generate unique and distinct tone qualities. The insertion of a mute needs to be indicated in both the score and parts at the end of the phrase prior to their use. Remember to give the player plenty of time to make any mute change by writing rests into the part. The three most common trumpet mutes are the Harmon mute, the cup mute, and the straight mute.

The Harmon mute has an adjustable stem which is usually removed in a jazz setting. This mute alters the trumpet tone into a much more focused, buzzy sound. The best example of the Harmon mute can be heard in many of Miles Davis' recordings. This mute requires an abundance of breath support since the mute blocks all the air from the bell of the horn, forcing it through the mute. The cup mute, on the other hand, provides a rounder, more mellow sound than the Harmon mute. For a good example of cup mute playing, listen to Miles Davis' 1954 recording of "Solar" on the album *Walkin'*. The straight mute produces a brighter, more nasal sound and is associated with a more dated repertoire such as Glenn Miller's "String of Pearls."

The Trombone

As with the trumpet, the arranger must understand the physical properties of the trombone in order to write for it successfully. The trombonist, like his trumpet-playing counterpart, manipulates his or her embouchure in order to sound the various partials of the overtone series. On a trumpet, the length of the tubing is changed by opening up extra segments of the instrument by pressing a valve. But on a trombone, the player changes the length of the instrument's tubing in a much more direct fashion—by moving the slide in or out with the hand. The trombone, like the trumpet, gets its bright sound from the primarily cylindrical bore, although because of it's lower range and larger size, it is also capable of producing warm and romantic lines. The trombone is sometimes referred to as a big, low-sounding trumpet because they share the same bore properties.

Slide Positions and Technical Facility

It is important to be aware of the pitches associated with each slide position. Some lines that look simple to play on paper might be extremely awkward on the trombone. For instance, moving between seventh position (slide fully extended) and first position (slide fully retracted) is obviously going to be problematic for the player. On the other hand, in the high tessitura of the trombone, all the notes can be played with only the first three positions. As a result, playing in this region is technically easier because the movements of the slide cover less distance.

The chart seen below shows the slide positions of each note on the trombone. The first three notes are known as *pedal tones*. After the pedal tones, the trombone moves through the slide positions beginning on a low E and continues up to the F above the staff. Notes above the F have been omitted because they are played with short slide positions that are easily negotiated by the player.

Trombone Range

Jazz trombone music is almost exclusively written in bass clef. Since the trombone is a nontransposing instrument, it is unnecessary to indicate a transposed range.

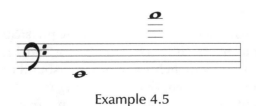

Example 4.5

The Registers of the Trombone

The lower notes of the trombone range are more difficult to control, as we saw with the trumpet. As the range moves into the middle and upper parts of the staff, the instrument's tone becomes more centered, and it will blend easily with other instruments. The dynamic range is wide in this part of the range. The notes above the staff result in a clear tone, and since the positions are closer together, they can be played more rapidly. One of the most common instrumentation errors I see is the writing of trombone parts that are too low. Writing on the top of the bass clef staff, and just above, works very well in small groups. Again, as with the trumpet, writing at the top of the range requires rest time for the player, as this is physically demanding. Playing soft passages is also difficult in the upper register.

Trombone Mutes

Trombone mutes can provide new tone colors for the jazz ensemble. The three most common mutes used by the trombone are the straight mute, the cup mute, and the bucket mute. The straight mute and cup mute both produce a nasal tone (the straight mute more so than the cup mute) while the bucket mute mellows the sound considerably.

 As with the trumpet, the insertion of a trombone mute needs to be indicated in both score and parts at the end of the phrase prior to their use. Remember to give the player plenty of time to make any mute change by writing rests into the part.

The Saxophone

The most commonly used saxophones are the alto, tenor and baritone saxes, although the soprano saxophone is also an important jazz instrument. Since every member of the saxophone family uses exactly the same fingerings, saxophone players often play more than one variety of saxophone. However, most players have a favorite type of saxophone on which they feel the most comfortable. The saxophone is an ideal instrument for melodies and countermelodies, and also background sustained parts.

Saxophone Transposition

Saxophones are built as either E♭ or B♭ instruments. The alto and baritone saxophones are E♭ instruments while the tenor and soprano saxophones are B♭ instruments. Saxophone music is notated in the treble clef, although some textbooks (including this one) often display the concert pitch of tenor and baritone saxophone parts in bass clef to avoid ledger lines. Music written for the alto saxophone must be transposed up a major sixth from concert pitch. Transposing the key signature is accomplished by adding three sharps or subtracting three flats from the written key signature.

 The example below shows the transposition of pitches and keys necessary when writing for the alto saxophone.

Example 4.6

Music written for the tenor saxophone must be transposed up a major ninth from concert pitch. Transposing the key signature is accomplished by adding two sharps or subtracting two flats from the written key signature as seen below.

Example 4.7

Music written for the baritone saxophone must be transposed up a major thirteenth (an octave and a sixth) from concert pitch. Transposing the key signature is accomplished by adding three sharps or subtracting three flats from the written key signature in the same way as is done for the alto saxophone.

Example 4.8

Although the baritone sax is a wonderful horn to include in small group writing, the suggested instrumentation for this text does not include this particular instrument. However, in a four-voice texture, it could certainly take the place of the trombone.

Saxophone Ranges

The next example illustrates the practical ranges of the alto, tenor and baritone saxophones. Keep in mind that not all saxophones are created equal as far as range is concerned. Although every saxophone uses the same fingerings, not all instruments have the same keys to press. Many (but not all) baritone saxophones are equipped with a low A key which extends the range of the instrument downward by a half step. And most saxophones made today have a high F♯ key that many older saxophones do not have. Here is a chart that shows the range of the saxophones.

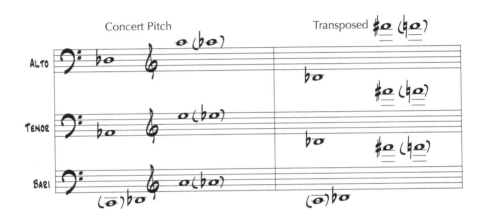

Example 4.9

The Registers of the Saxophone

The lowest notes of the saxophone (below a low transposed C♯) can be quite difficult to control, especially by a less experienced player. In the staff, the saxophone's tone is rich and full, making this range a very often-used area for arrangers seeking to write sustained chords. The tone of the saxophone becomes more strident as it ascends to the top of the staff and above the staff, giving the saxophone tone a bit more projection in this tessitura. Above the staff, the tone of the saxophone can become very bright and loud—and also difficult to control. These notes of the saxophone, especially above a high C, can also go sharp, making intonation a challenge for players of all levels.

As mentioned previously, the top note of the normal saxophone range is the written F♯, or written F if the instrument does not have a high F♯ key. The advanced saxophonist, however, is not limited to this range. With specialized fingerings and alterations to the airstream, the saxophonist may play upward into the altissimo register (the extremely high notes above the normal range of the saxophone). Because a player must be quite advanced to have adequate control over the altissimo register, even experienced arrangers never write in this range of the saxophone.

Chapter Summary

1. An instrument's tone quality is the product of factors such as the material from which it is constructed, the shape of its bore, the presence or absence of overtones, and its method of tone production.
2. Arrangers must memorize the ranges of the instruments.
3. Combining instruments within the same family, or with a similar timbre or range creates a homogeneous sound.
4. Combining instruments from different families with a different timbre or range creates a contrasting sound.
5. The power and bright tone of the trumpet make it a natural melodic instrument.
6. Endurance and range are the two most important considerations when writing for trumpet.
7. The trombone can produce a bright sound similar to the trumpet, but also can sound warm and mellow.
8. The slide positions of the trombone affect the facility of the instrument; changing positions quickly works best with slide positions that are adjacent to one another.
9. Trombone and trumpet mutes create new instrumental colors.
10. The saxophone works well as a melodic instrument, but also in background sustained parts.
11. All the members of the saxophone family use the same fingerings.

Assignment 4.1

Transposition

In the staff provided on the next page, transpose the given melody for trumpet, alto sax, tenor sax, baritone sax, and trombone. Notate the trombone and baritone sax parts one octave down from concert pitch. Do not change the octave of the trumpet, alto sax, or tenor sax.

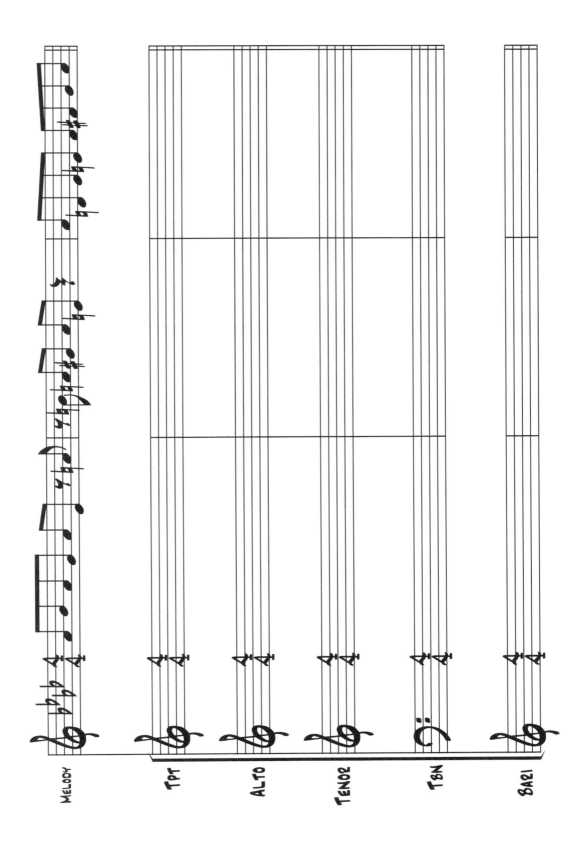

The Rhythm Section

The instruments of the rhythm section are piano, guitar, bass, and drums. Arrangers who play wind instruments often struggle with these instruments both in terms of notation and understanding their individual roles within the ensemble. Rhythm section players employ much more improvisation than other members of the ensemble. For this reason, this part of the ensemble demands a flexible and unique method of notation and also a certain level of detachment from the arranger. For instance, the pianist, guitarist, and bassist are usually only reading chord symbols, and the drummer may have long sections of just timekeeping with virtually no notation.

Role in the Ensemble

Including the word "rhythm" in the name of the "rhythm section" emphasizes the element of time-keeping. This section, however, also provides the harmonic framework. Melodies can also be performed by pianists, guitarists, and even bassists. While these three elements can be specifically notated by the arranger, the section usually improvises and "comps" their parts.

The Basso Continuo

The practice of using a group of musicians to supply the rhythmic and harmonic foundation for a larger ensemble is not new. During the Baroque period, the "rhythm section" was called the *basso continuo*. The written music for the basso continuo consisted of a notated bass line with special numbers below the bass notes. The numbers in each measure were special chord symbols called *figured bass* that a musician playing a chordal instrument would use to improvise (or *realize*, to use the appropriate term) a chordal accompaniment. These chords would be played by a harpsichord, lute, or some other instrument. The bass line itself would be played by a bass instrument such as a bassoon or viola da gamba. The usage of figured bass allowed musicians to improvise a chordal accompaniment within specific parameters. The jazz rhythm section of today provides the bass line and chords much in the same way as the basso continuo of the Baroque era.

The word *comping* is short for "accompaniment." When comping, the rhythm section players exercise a large degree of freedom over what they play. The voicings in the piano and guitar, the bass lines, and drum timekeeping are all improvised, but within the organization of the arrangement. Often the players require only chord symbols with slashes representing the duration of each chord. When rhythm section players are required to add something specific, appropriate notation is blended into the part. The arranger must not overnotate rhythm section parts. Young arrangers must realize that the players themselves may be able to provide better solutions to specific voicings and styles than the arranger could.

As mentioned above, simple slashes are used to indicate comping. As long as the style and tempo are indicated, most players should be able to provide an appropriate accompaniment. Also, experienced rhythm section members play differently during the melody than during solo sections. In a swing tune, when playing the head, the rhythm section may want to play with a "two" feel—that's when the drummer and bassist emphasize the first and third beats of a 4/4 measure with the bassist playing mainly roots and fifths. After the head the rhythm section will normally play in "four" and the bassist will begin to play a quarter note bass line. Rhythm section performance practice is beyond the focus of this text, but simply knowing the difference between a "two" feel and a "four" feel will be enough for most beginning arrangers. The arranger can indicate which feel is appropriate for the rhythm section, but often the players themselves will make the decision if nothing is indicated.

Notating Rhythm Section Parts

I've observed that while rhythm section musicians transition quite well to writing for horn players, wind players often struggle with the notation of rhythm section parts. In reality, these parts are actually very simple to write. Two important notation methods are described below.

Comping

Below is an example of a score which indicates comping for piano, bass, and drums accompanying the melody of "Why Not Now." Notice that each member of the rhythm section has only the following in his or her part: the time-feel (where it says "in two"), slashes, and chord symbols—the rest is left up to the player.

Example 5.1

Rhythmic Notation

To notate a specific rhythm for the entire rhythm section, use large note heads with no identifiable pitch. This type of notation is called *rhythmic notation*. If you want the pianist to voice the chord with a specific note on the top, simply write the desired note on the staff with the chord symbol and include the instruction "Voice with note on top."

If you have something precise in mind for any of the instruments, provide the exact notation. It is very common to blend actual notes with slash notation and rhythmic notation. Keep in mind, however, that the players themselves might have a better idea of what to play in that particular spot than you do.

The next example illustrates a score using the same instruments accompanying the identical section of "Why Not Now" as shown in example 5.1. Slashes, rhythmic notation, and exact notation are blended together. This uncharacteristic example is for educational purposes only since most charts will not include this much variety of notation in such a short span.

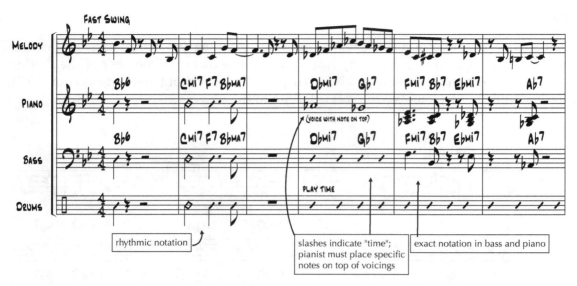

Example 5.2

The Instruments of the Rhythm Section

The arranger must understand the dramatic differences among the instruments of the rhythm section. In the trumpet section, everybody is holding a trumpet. In the trombone section, everyone (hopefully) is holding a trombone. But in the rhythm section, there are four completely different instruments playing together. The following pages serve only as an introduction to the instruments of the rhythm section. Consult instrument-specific method books for more detailed information or ask for input from rhythm section musicians.

Piano

The pianist plays a crucial role in the small group. Duties such as voicing the various chords, comping behind soloists, and integrating with the bass and drums all fall to the pianist. The pianist should be able to choose an appropriate tessitura in which to play his or her chord voicings and should also be aware of the amount of rhythmic complexity injected into the fabric of the arrangement. A good adage for pianists in comping situations is "less is more."

Also, the pianist is responsible for dictating much of the style of the piece. The pianist could play heavy "McCoy Tyner" voicings that use a lot of fourths or perhaps use a more sparse "Count Basie" approach to comping. This helps to set the tone of the entire arrangement.

Piano parts are often notated on one staff rather than on the more space-consuming grand staff, particularly when only chord changes are indicated. However, sometimes both one and two staves are necessary in different sections of the arrangement. Fortunately, computer notation programs are able to score the piano part both ways, thereby saving valuable space. Using only one staff when possible will prevent you from handing your pianist a part that is ten pages long!

Guitar

While the guitar is not included in the musical examples in this text, it is frequently used in jazz rhythm sections. The following tips will help you write successfully for guitar:

1. The guitar sounds an octave lower than written.
2. The guitar serves as a wonderful companion timbre to wind instruments; it is often scored in unison (or octave) lines doubling other members of the ensemble.
3. Don't assume that something that works on piano will also work on the guitar. These two instruments function very differently.

The pianist and guitarist should not comp chords at the same time. Chord symbols can be interpreted in a variety of ways, and the pianist and guitarist need to avoid playing conflicting voicings and rhythms. Experienced pianists and guitarists pay close attention to if and how they are blending—and without written or verbal instructions they will decide among themselves which player will comp chords while the other rests. For instance, during a horn solo, the pianist and guitarist will often take turns comping chords behind the soloist.

Bass

The bass sounds an octave lower than written. The bass range illustrated below is for a four-string instrument (some electric basses have a fifth string). The strings are tuned to E, A, D, and G. Typically, the acoustic upright bass is found in more traditional jazz settings with other acoustic instruments. The electric bass is most effective in the jazz/rock fusion idiom, paired with other electric instruments, such as electric piano and/or guitar.

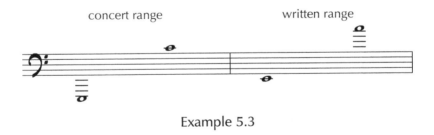

Example 5.3

The bass player should be viewed as both the timekeeper and provider of the underlying style and harmonic foundation. In a small group setting, the bassist sometimes reinforces the pianist's left hand during ostinato passages. During normal timekeeping sections, however, the pianist should not interfere with the bassist's comping pattern.

Drum Set

The drummer's most important responsibility is timekeeping. Much of the success of your arrangement depends upon how it feels to the listener, and the drummer is responsible for this important aspect of small group playing. In fact, the manner in which the members of the rhythm section interact with one another is critical to all jazz performances.

Drum Notation

Notating drum parts for small jazz ensembles should not be overly complicated. Your job as arranger is to notate the parts as clearly as possible, creating an appropriate balance of both structure and freedom for the players. All of the players in small jazz groups need to listen intently to one another, and an elaborate drum part can distract the drummer from his or her primary goal—interacting with the band.

   Fortunately, there are simple ways to notate drum parts:

1. Slash notation
2. Background figures
3. Rhythmic notation

Slash Notation

Slash notation (seen below) refers to diagonal slashes placed in the middle of the staff. This notation obviously gives the player the most freedom to interact with the other musicians and to provide his or her own interpretation.

Example 5.4

   There is a lot of information contained in example 5.4. The tempo/style marking indicates that this will be a fast swing tune and the drummer should begin the chart rather aggressively because of the forte marking. He or she should also play the part with sticks rather than with brushes or mallets. There is also a two-bar repeat. This is a space-saving device that says to the player, "repeat the previous two bars."

Background Figures

The drummer is often asked to support parts being played by the horns while simultaneously keeping the time moving. These background figures are indicated with small note heads, with stems pointing up, placed above the staff containing slash notation. These rhythms are then played on either drums or cymbals at the drummer's discretion. It is often helpful to provide written instructions identifying the instruments to be supported along with articulations. This type of notation is illustrated on the following page.

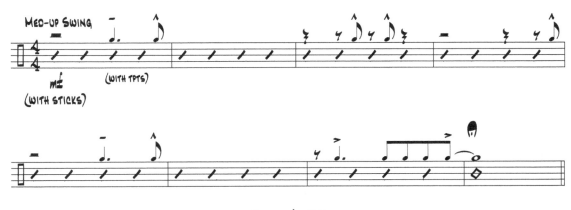

Example 5.5

Rhythmic Notation

Often the drummer is asked to reinforce the entire ensemble with kicks. Rhythmic notation is indicated by simply notating the rhythm on the middle line of the staff with large note heads. This type of notation is illustrated below. Along with the figures, the drummer would also provide the time, blending the kicks with the basic feel of the tune. This type of notation was also seen above in example 5.2, because all rhythm section members read this type of notation.

Example 5.6

Reinforcement and Integration

Reinforcement of the horns is a role shared to varying degrees by all the members of the rhythm section, and balancing timekeeping with support of the horns is an important decision for arrangers. Too much integration (particularly during background sections of solos) can make the chart lose momentum. Conversely, if the rhythm section offers no support of the horns, the band will not be working together as a unit.

You may want to take a moment and examine a few sections of the complete arrangements in chapter 17 focusing on the rhythm section. Observe how slash notation is blended with actual notation in the piano, bass, and drum parts.

Don't Be Intimidated by the Rhythm Section!

If you are a wind player and are able to perform with a fine rhythm section, use the opportunity to observe what each player is doing. Also, seek the advice of rhythm section members. Finally, study scores that provide a balance between the arranger's wishes and the freedom of the rhythm section members to add their own interpretation. If successful, the result will be a spontaneous and creative final product.

Chapter Summary

1. The rhythm section provides the harmonic and rhythmic foundation of the ensemble.
2. Rhythm section notation is quite different from wind instrument notation.
3. Slash notation, which indicates timekeeping, is the most common notational device.
4. Arrangements should provide a balance of improvised rhythm section parts and specific notation.

Assignment 5.1

Rhythm Section Parts

On the next two pages there is an incomplete score for a small group chart. Only the melody is given in the top staff. Your assignment is to notate appropriate piano, bass, and drum parts to accompany the melody. In the parts you create, include the following elements:

- PIANO: Notate slashes in measures 1–6 and in measure 9; rhythmic notation based on the rhythm of the melody in measures 7–8 and 10–11. Notate the chord symbols. Write the same notation in both clefs, but put the chord symbols above the treble clef staff.

- BASS: Same as piano, but write the roots of the chords where rhythmic notation occurs. Remember to notate the chord symbols.

- DRUMS: Notate slashes in the measures 1–9. Use background figure notation in measures 8–9. Use rhythmic notation in measures 10–11 based on the rhythm of the melody.

Don't forget to include time signatures for all parts and key signatures for piano and bass. Indicate "medium swing" as the tempo/style.

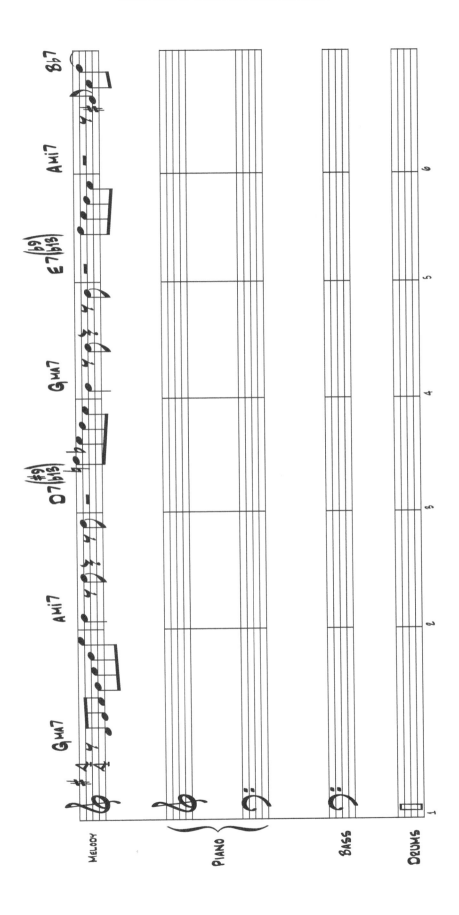

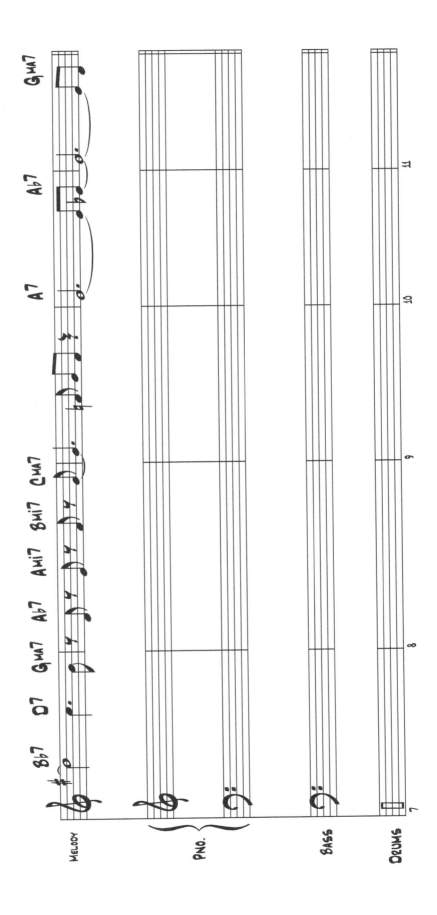

Part III

Jazz Harmony & Voicings

Successful jazz musicians are usually excellent music theorists. While improvisers and arrangers may have different approaches and labels for various concepts, most of them have an understanding of jazz harmony and chord voicings. Also, since not every melodic note is a chord member, an understanding of nonharmonic tone treatment is vital for jazz musicians. We will find in part III that these concepts are interwoven, and therefore the various voicing types and nonharmonic tone treatments will be presented as a unit.

The term *voicing* refers to the distribution of chord tones. A chord can be voiced with as few as two notes (e.g the third and seventh) or can contain all of the possible chord tones including the upper extensions.

Part III is divided into the following four chapters:

Chapter 6: Tertian harmony
Chapter 7: Quartal harmony
Chapter 8: Slash chords
Chapter 9: Nonharmonic Tones

Whether you are arranging for two horns or for the thirteen horns of the typical big band, keeping these three types of voicings in mind as well as the approach techniques covered in chapter 9 will help to organize your thinking about jazz harmony.

Tertian Harmony

Tertian (pronounced *TURR-shin*) harmony will be familiar to anyone who has studied harmony in a basic music theory course. Tertian harmony is built by stacking notes in thirds. The simplest tertian structure is the triad. The word *triad* comes from the Greek word that means "three." The three notes in a triad are the root, the third and the fifth of the chord. If you continue to stack notes in thirds beyond the triad, the chord becomes more complex and additional information is needed to indicate the quality of that chord. The number next to the chord symbol identifies the top note. Observe what happens when we stack a chord higher and higher in thirds:

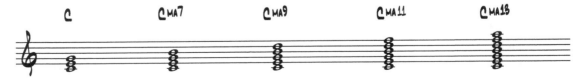

Example 6.1

The tones above the seventh are called the *upper extensions*. Keep in mind that you may not extend a chord beyond the thirteenth. If you continued to stack notes in thirds above the thirteenth, the chord tones would begin to repeat themselves.

Most jazz chords are labeled as some kind of seventh chord (e.g., Cma7). The tones of a seventh chord are the root, third, fifth, and seventh. Here are a few examples of typical seventh chords:

Example 6.2

Close and Open Voicings

As we distribute chord tones (or "voice" them) we can either stack them consecutively, as is illustrated above, or we can create gaps between some of the chord tones. Chords that are stacked consecutively within the range of one octave are said to be in a *close voicing*. If the chord has four different tones, it is commonly referred to as *four-way close*. Chords that are not consecutively stacked and exceed the interval of one octave are said to be in *open voicing*. Tackling close voicings first will make the open voicing section of the chapter much simpler to understand.

Four-Way Close Voicings

As mentioned above, a chord containing four separate notes that reside within the range of an octave is called *four-way close*. This voicing is the most common structure used by jazz arrangers and pianists because it works well in harmonizing fast-moving lines but can also provide the harmonic foundation for lush ballads.

Chord Tone Substitutions

Most chords in the jazz idiom are expressed simply by indicating three things: the root, the quality of the chord, and the number seven. A seasoned jazz performer can embellish that basic chord symbol by adding and/or changing chord tones to express a richer, more colorful sound. These musicians understand that the seventh chord designation is merely a point of departure and that upper extensions, as well as the fourth and sixth, play a vital role in jazz harmony. Simple root position seventh chords that have only the fundamental tones (i.e., the root, third, fifth, and seventh) are actually the exception rather than the rule.

The richness of jazz harmony involves a hierarchy of substitution possibilities for these four tones. For this reason, it is best to think of each of these chord tones not as required tones, as you may be led to believe from the chord symbol, but rather as chord tones that are almost always replaced, or substituted, according to rather specific rules. Let's first pair each of these fundamental chord tones with possible substitutions, illustrated below:

- The root can be replaced by the ninth.
- The third can be replaced by the fourth.
- The fifth can be replaced by the thirteenth or eleventh.
- The seventh can be replaced by the sixth.

I mentioned above that there are rules regarding these substitution possibilities, and these rules are dependent upon three important considerations: the chord quality, the key that you're in, and the tone color you want. We'll discuss how keys affect the substitution rules in a moment. First let's explore chord tone substitutions in the context of chord quality and tone color.

The upper extensions, along with the fourth and sixth, are all major intervals above the root (in the case of the ninth, sixth, and thirteenth) or perfect intervals (in the case of the fourth and eleventh). However, the chord symbol can indicate alterations of these tones (i.e., ♯11). Ninths can be lowered or raised, elevenths can be raised, but not lowered (a flatted eleventh is the equivalent of a major third), and thirteenths can be lowered but not raised (a raised thirteenth is the equivalent of a minor seventh). Also, the thirteenth and sixth are the same note an octave apart, as are the eleventh and fourth. With this background knowledge, examine the chart on the next page listing chord tone substitutions for ma7, dom7, mi7, mi7(♭5), and diminished 7 chords. You'll notice that even though the ninth, eleventh, and thirteenth are considered upper extensions (i.e., above the seventh) they are notated in the same octave as the fundamental chord tones.

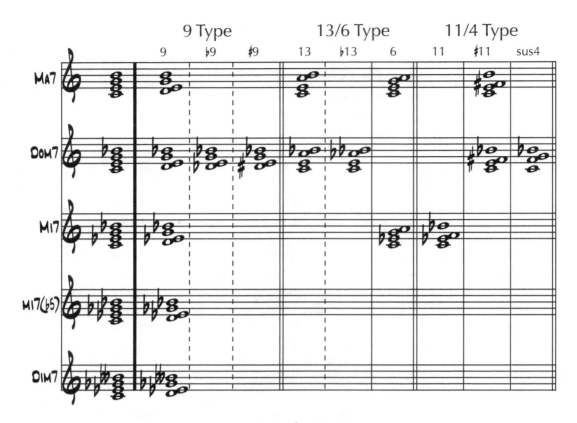

Example 6.3

The chart seen above lists three possible substitution types:

1. ninths
2. thirteenths/sixths
3. elevenths/fourths

By reading the chart from left to right, the following points can be summarized:

- Ninths can replace the root in all chord qualities.
- Raised and lowered ninths can replace the root only in a dom7.
- Thirteenths can replace the fifth in a ma7 and a dom7.
- Flatted thirteenths can replace the fifth only in a dom7.
- Sixths can replace the seventh in a ma7 and a min7.
- Elevenths can replace the fifth only in a mi7.
- Raised elevenths can replace the fifth in a ma7 and a dom7 and are sometimes labeled as flatted fifths, e.g., Cma7(♭5).
- The suspended fourth can replace the third only in a dom7.
- Dim 7ths are unique, since they are symmetrical; a note placed a whole step above any of the chord tones functions as a ninth.

All of this begs the question: Why use these particular substitutions? When should I use a thirteenth? Should I use it in conjunction with a ninth? An altered ninth? As was mentioned above, chord tone substitutions provide a richer, more colorful sound. They also provide more dissonance, and *dissonant chords tend to drive the music forward toward a resolution.* For example, the dominant seventh chord, when functioning as a V chord (which is its usual role) requires—yes that's a strong word—substitute chord tones, because the chord needs a degree of instability as it leads to a resolution. The thirteenth provides that dissonance, as it clashes (in a good way) with the seventh, because the thirteenth and seventh are only a half step from one another. Later in this chapter we'll be revisiting chord tone substitution when jazz chord positions are discussed, and we'll see how these various substitutions are combined. For now, however, we need to briefly discuss how keys and functional harmony affect substitution choices.

An Important Consideration: What Key Are You In?

The substitution chart above is quite concise in summarizing the substitution options. However, it does contain one unavoidable flaw—the tonality of both the overall key or the "key of the moment" (involving secondary function) is not taken into consideration. For example, the thirteenth of a V chord (with a chord root of G) in the key of C minor will be a flat thirteenth (an E♭) to match the key. So the tonality will govern what you utilize as substitutes. This, however, actually makes things easier. The key provides a structure that guides the arranger toward particular decisions. This will become clear as you read and study the section on the ii–V–I progression below.

Important!

Keep in mind that in a jazz standard, chord symbols are merely points of departure—while a symbol may call for only a seventh, the arranger has the freedom to choose appropriate substitutions. This is, in fact, a big part of the arranger's job description.

Inversions and Positions

We learn in music theory classes that chords may be inverted so that a note other than the root serves as the lowest tone. Therefore a triad may be arranged with any of its three notes as the lowest note for a total of three possible positions. Since a seventh chord has four notes, it may be arranged with any of its four notes as the lowest note, for a total of four possible positions, as demonstrated on the following page:

Example 6.4

Notice what's happening here: the chord is simply rearranged or inverted, but the order of the chord tones always stays the same. The bottom note is simply shifted to the top of the chord as the positions move from left to right. The chart below illustrates yet another way to view this phenomenon:

Seventh Chord Positions

Position	Chord Tones, Listed From Bottom to Top
Root Position	Root, 3, 5, 7
First Inversion	3, 5, 7, Root
Second Inversion	5, 7, Root, 3
Third Inversion	7, Root, 3, 5

One good way to familiarize yourself with chord positions is to play them on the piano. As you play these chords you will be able to see, hear and feel them all at once.

Jazz Chord Positions

Our next step toward understanding voicing techniques is to make the connection between chord position and possible chord tone substitutions. Jazz theorists apply letter name labels to denote positions (unfortunately with a certain degree of inconsistency and ambiguity). As mentioned above, there are four positions of a four-note chord. Many jazz piano method books refer to only two positions: the "A" position (in which the third is the bottom note) and the "B" position (in which the seventh is the bottom note). Why do these method books identify only two rather than four possibilities? These positions place the most active tones (the third and seventh) on the bottom of the chord structure leading to very smooth movement of chord tones from one chord to the next, otherwise known as *voice leading*. There are two other possible positions, however, and I have chosen to label them "C" and "D" as seen in the chart on the following page. Notice that I've included some of the substitution possibilities discussed earlier, namely the ninth and thirteenth.

A Position			B Position				C Position			D Position		
CMA7	CMI7	C7	CMA7	CMI7	C7	w/o 13th C7	CMA7	CMI7	C7	CMA7	CMI7	C7
9	9	9	5	5	13	5	7	7	7	3	3	3
7	7	7	3	3	3	3	5	5	5	9	root	9
5	5	13	9	9	9	9	3	3	3	7	7	7
3	3	3	7	7	7	7	9	9	9	5	5	5

Example 6.5

The chart seen above reveals small differences among the chord positions. Recall that the thirteenth may replace the fifth in dominant seventh chords in order to increase the dissonance of this important chord. This is seen in the A and B positions. The dissonance between the thirteenth and seventh is very characteristic of jazz harmony. However, the B position offers the option of using the thirteenth or the fifth because there is enough dissonance between the third and ninth (the E and D) in the middle of the chord to give it a jazz flavor. Finally, notice the use of the root instead of the ninth in the D position of the minor seventh. The ninth would create a half step interval with the minor third (a D with an Eb) on top of the chord, which is something to avoid under normal circumstances.

There are two important points that I would like to reemphasize:

1. Do not place a minor second immediately below the melody note as this will obscure it. A major second will work (see the major and dominant chords in the D position), but it still results in a dissonance next to the melody. Use with care.
2. Inner-chord clusters are desirable in certain circumstances, especially on chords with a dominant function. However, avoid two groups of clusters. For this reason, the fifth is used rather than the thirteenth in the D position of the dominant seventh in example 6.5.

The Value of the Piano for Arranging Students

Most jazz arrangers spend time at the piano keyboard trying out voicings and exploring the ways in which tones move in and out of the prevailing harmony. While viewing music notation on the staff has certain advantages over playing the same notation on the keyboard (for example, a Gb and F♯ look the same on a keyboard but are separate notes on the staff), the keyboard allows us to see and hear voicings, scales, melodies, and voice-leading with a level of clarity not possible by looking merely at music notation.

Shell Voicings

Shell voicings are three-note structures that contain the third, seventh, and one additional tone, usually the fifth or ninth. If you've not played piano voicings before taking up this book, these simple structures are a good place to start. Example 6.6 illustrates major, minor, and dominant chords voiced in A and B positions. Play them in your right hand with the chord roots in your left and practice them in all keys. Use the circle of fifths to move through every chord (i.e., C–F–B♭–E♭–A♭–D♭–G♭–B–E–A–D–G). Play one chord quality and position at a time—for example, all major sevenths in A position around the circle.

Example 6.6

After you feel comfortable with these shell voicings, try playing them in four-way close by adding the missing tone. For example, the A position Cma7 above is missing the fifth. Refer to the voicings illustrated in example 6.5 to guide you. Again, play one chord quality at a time (i.e., all major sevenths in A position, etc.).

Assignment 6.1

Four-Way Close Voicings

In the staves provided on the next two pages, notate the chords with four-way close voicings. The top note is given; you must add the lower three tones. Though these chords are not actually in a key, use chord tone substitutions at your discretion. The first one is completed for you.

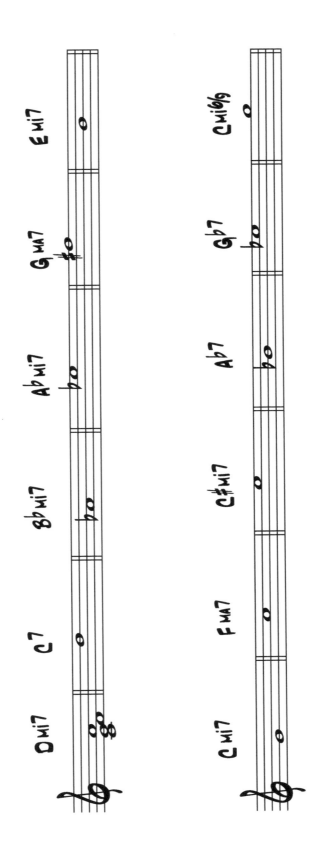

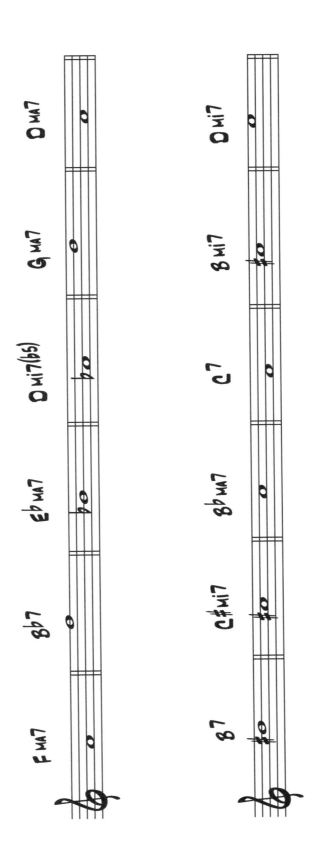

Assignment 6.2

Four-Way Close Voicings II

In the staves on the following pages, notate each chord with four-way close voicings under the given melody note; then distribute the notes on the grand staff using SATB format. "SATB" refers to voices and the stem directions differentiating each voice. From top down on the treble clef staff: soprano, stems up; alto, stems down. From top down on the bass clef staff: tenor, stems up; bass, stems down. Though these chords are not actually in a key, use chord tone substitutions at your discretion. The first voicing is done for you.

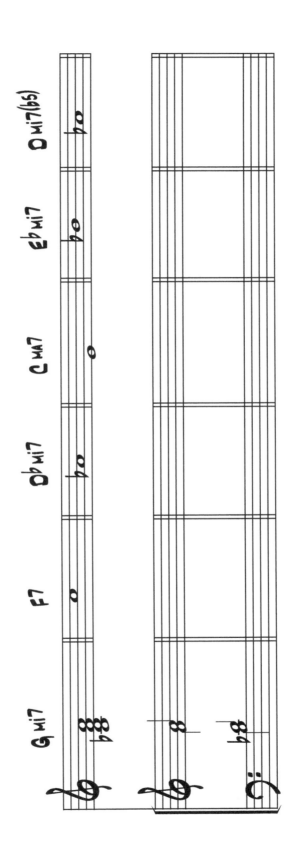

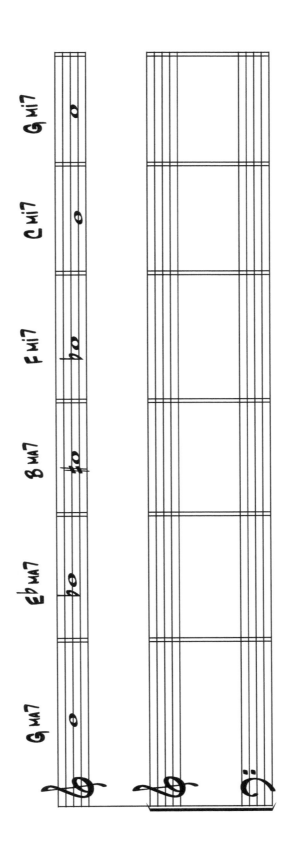

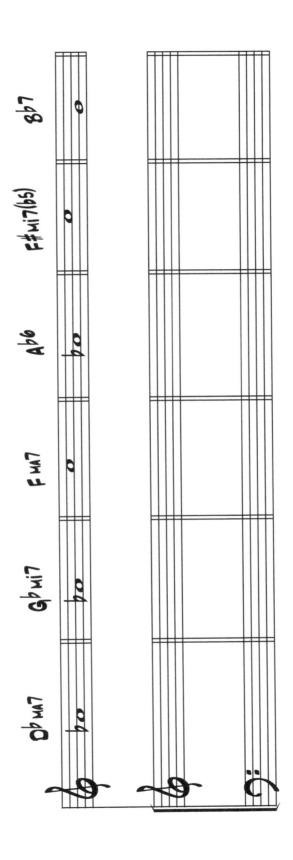

Assignment 6.3

Four-Way Close Voicings III

Voice the following chords with four-way close voicings. Use the indicated key for each chord as you determine which chord tone substitutions to use. Some substitutions are suggested by the chord symbol. Notate them in SATB format on the condensed score grand staff. The top note is given. Transfer the voicing from the "condensed voicing" grand staff to the instruments below. *Write a transposed score.* The first one is completed for you.

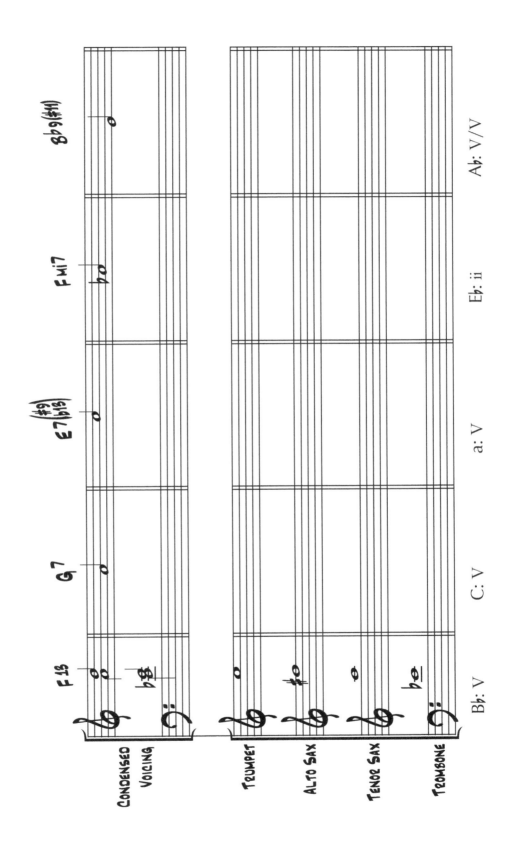

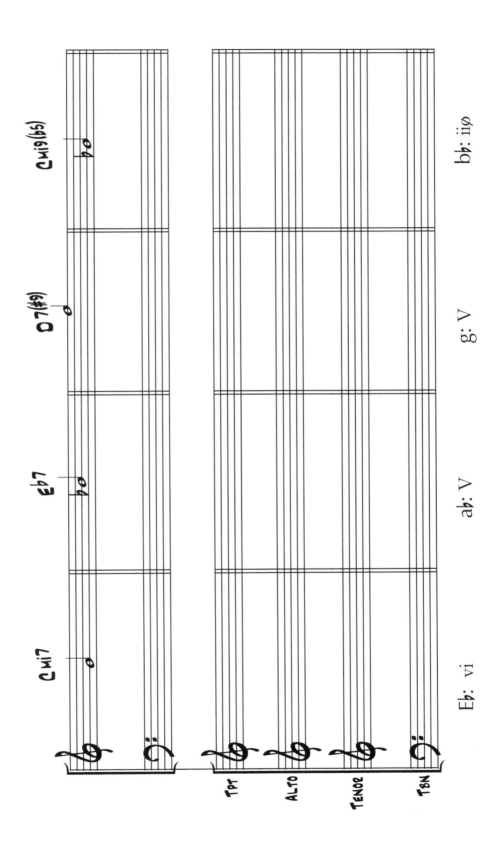

Circle of Fifths Progressions

The A and B positions are the most commonly used inversions when voicing chords for comping. These particular positions work especially well in circle of fifths progressions because the active tones (the third and seventh) are on the bottom of the harmony. The two positions alternate as the progression moves around the circle, thereby creating the smoothest possible voice leading.

Example 6.7 contains another keyboard exercise and also serves as a useful visual illustration of circle of fifths motion. The example shows major seventh shell voicings moving between the A and B positions, illustrating smooth voice leading. While only the first four chords of the circle of fifths are notated, play them all the way around the circle. Note how the voices move: thirds and sevenths move in the same voice and alternate with one another. The fifths and ninths also alternate with one another. Practice minor seventh and dominant seventh chords in the same manner.

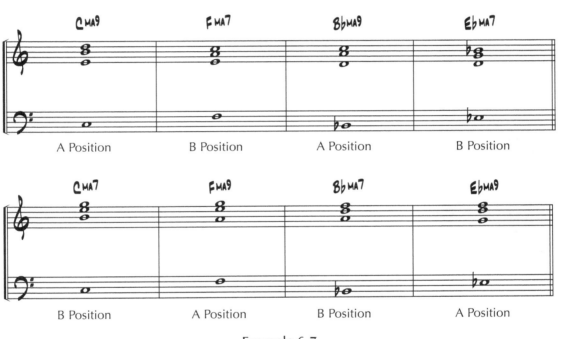

Example 6.7

As in the previous keyboard exercise, try these in four-way close position. Example 6.8 illustrates this motion. The chord tone motion described above holds true here as well—thirds and sevenths alternate, as do fifths and ninths. Note that these are all notated as ma7 chords; recall that the ninth is a substitute for the root and is often not indicated in the symbol.

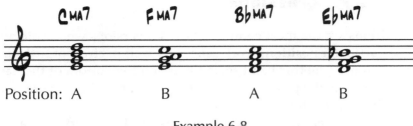

Position: A   B   A   B

Example 6.8

The ii–V–I Progression

The extremely common ii–V–I progression provides an excellent opportunity to study the various voice leading procedures used by the jazz arranger and how tonality can affect chord tone substitutions. As we saw demonstrated in the example above, the positions of the chords alternate between A and B because the ii–V–I is a circle of fifths progression.

The example below contains the ii–V–I progression in both C major (first two measures) and C minor (last two measures). As you listen to the audio track of this example, notice the smoothness of the voice leading (the audio track has a bass line which is not notated in the example).

🔊 6.9

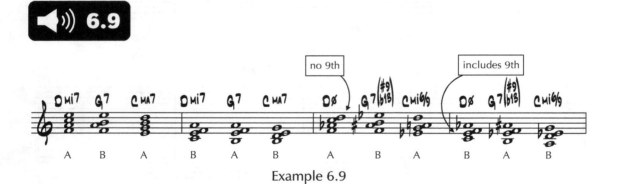

Example 6.9

ii–V–I Voice Leading

The chart on the following page expands upon example 6.9 by illustrating the movement of each chord tone in a ii–V–I chord progression using alternating A and B chord positions.

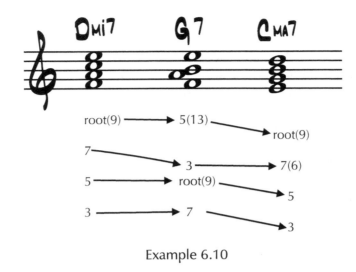

Example 6.10

Notice that the sevenths and thirds move in the same voice and alternate with one another, as was described above in the circle of fifths discussion. Roots (or ninths) and fifths (or thirteenths) also alternate with each other. So it's actually rather simple. The motion in each voice is identical if the progression were to begin with a B position ii chord. Also, the chart works for both major and minor keys, but there are some specific details about minor discussed below.

Minor Chord Progressions

While the voices in the minor progression move in a similar fashion to the major version, there are some complicating factors to consider. If you have studied traditional music theory and practiced minor scales on your instrument, you know that there are three minor scales: natural, harmonic, and melodic. Furthermore, there are modes derived from the ascending melodic minor scale that play an important role in jazz harmony. This provides a myriad of chord tone choices for jazz performers and arrangers when working in minor keys, and these choices are revealed in the ii$^\emptyset$–V–i progression in example 6.9. For example, the tonic minor is often harmonized with a sixth rather than a seventh. The sixth is derived from the melodic minor scale since it's a major sixth above the bass (e.g., in a Cmi6/9, the sixth is an A natural, even if you're in a key signature of C minor, which includes an A♭).

The ii and V chords in minor progressions are associated with particular modes of melodic minor. The ii$^\emptyset$ can include a major ninth above the bass note (the E voiced in the middle of the D$^\emptyset$ in the B position of example 6.9) which is a tone that is taken from Locrian ♯2—the sixth mode of melodic minor. The V chord contains tones that are part of the super Locrian mode—the seventh mode of melodic minor (e.g., the raised ninth and flatted thirteenth). Performing and arranging in minor keys can be confusing—but because this material is so important, arranging students must strive to thoroughly understand minor harmony and the modes of the melodic minor scale. I recall that after presenting these modes to a piano student, he stated, "That's what jazz sounds like."

More About the Sixth

As mentioned previously in the discussion of chord tone substitutions, the sixth is a common substitution for the seventh. This happens quite frequently at the end of many jazz standards in which the final chord calls for a major seventh yet the root of the chord is the melody note. Since the major seventh is only a half step below the melody, using a major seventh in that case would be too dissonant, particularly for the conclusion of a tune. The sixth is also used in conjunction with the ninth in the 6/9 quartal construction of major and minor chords (more about this in the next chapter). Finally, the sixth is always a major sixth above the root regardless of the key signature.

Piano Exercises for the ii–V–I Progression

Learning to play the ii–V–I progression on the piano in major and minor keys will help you both see and hear the voice leading. As you play them, notice how thirds alternate with sevenths, and fifths (or the substituted thirteenths) alternate with roots (or the substituted ninths). Understanding this motion is critical for arrangers. Play them in the same manner that you practiced the individual voicings above: right hand plays the chords, left hand plays the roots. The progression is notated with shell voicings in both major and minor in the example shown below. Practice them in all keys.

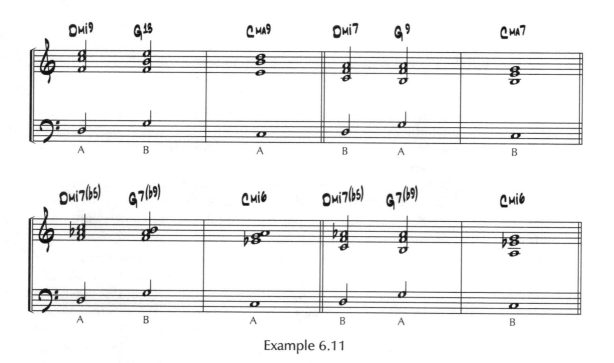

Example 6.11

Like the previous piano exercises, try these progressions in four-way close voicings. Think about the chart presented in example 6.10 as you observe how the tones move in each voice. These form the basis of the voice motion for much of what we'll be discussing as we move along.

The ii–V–I progression is the final keyboard exercise presented in this text. Obviously, these exercises only scratch the surface of jazz keyboard skills. The more facility you have as a pianist (even if it's not your primary instrument) the better you will understand the voice leading principles outlined throughout the text. Use the piano keyboard as much as possible as you examine the examples in subsequent chapters; it is a wonderful tool for arrangers.

Choosing a Chord Position

Choosing a four-way close chord position (either A, B, C, or D) to use at any particular point in an arrangement depends upon two factors: range and context. A simple rule of thumb regarding range is this: On the piano keyboard, close position chords sound best if notated between the D below middle C and the G above middle C, as shown below:

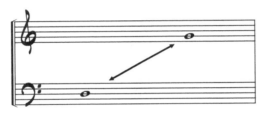

Example 6.12

Since chord tones often move in stepwise fashion (in circle progressions), each chord position will be determined by the previous one until range becomes a problem. The following example illustrates tertian voicings in one of the example pieces, "Why Not Now." Chord positions are labeled throughout. The tonic chord is a Bb6, rather than the more familiar Bbma7. The sixth, G, is present to prevent an unwanted dissonance with the first melody note (the Bb) especially for a tune with standard chord changes.

Example 6.13

Notice the flow of the voicing positions in example 6.13. When the chords move by step, the position stays the same, as between the Gb7 and Fmi7. When the chords move in a circle of fifths progression, as in the Cmi7 to F7 to Bbma7, the positions alternate. The chord movement of a third, between Bbma7 and Dbmi7, involves a change of position, although when moving in thirds either position causes virtually the same intervallic leap for all voices. In these cases, range is the most important factor in deciding on a position.

This next example, taken from the bridge of "Sabrosa," illustrates similar tendencies in chord movement. Notice that the melody dives down into the chord voicing in the fourth measure. This was done to keep the voicing in a satisfactory range.

Example 6.14

Once again the chords alternate positions when moving around the circle and remain in the same position when moving by step.

Assignment 6.4

The ii–V–I Progression

In the staves provided on the next two pages, notate the ii–V–I progression in major and minor for the requested keys. Use the A and B positions of four-way close voicings. The keys of F major and F minor are demonstrated first. Notice that the chord symbols are complete (i.e., every substitution is accounted for by the chord symbol); this is not always the case in "real" music. For this assignment, make the chord symbol reflect all chord tone substitutions present in the voicing.

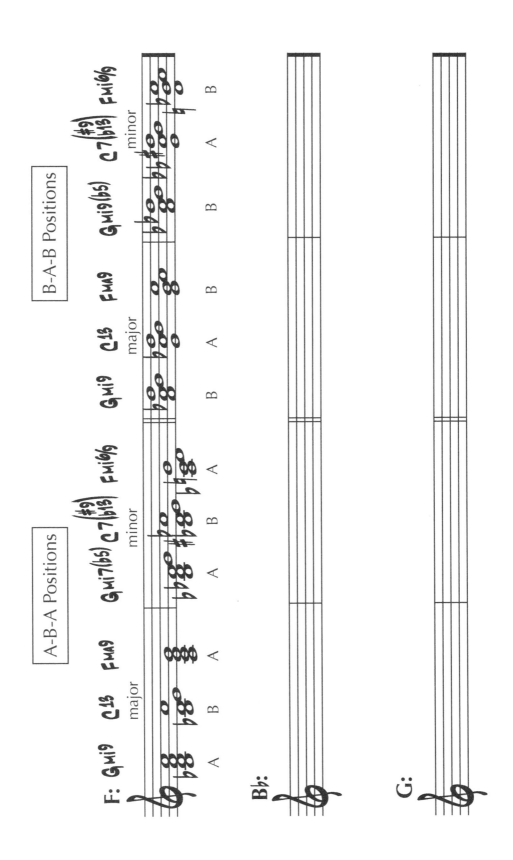

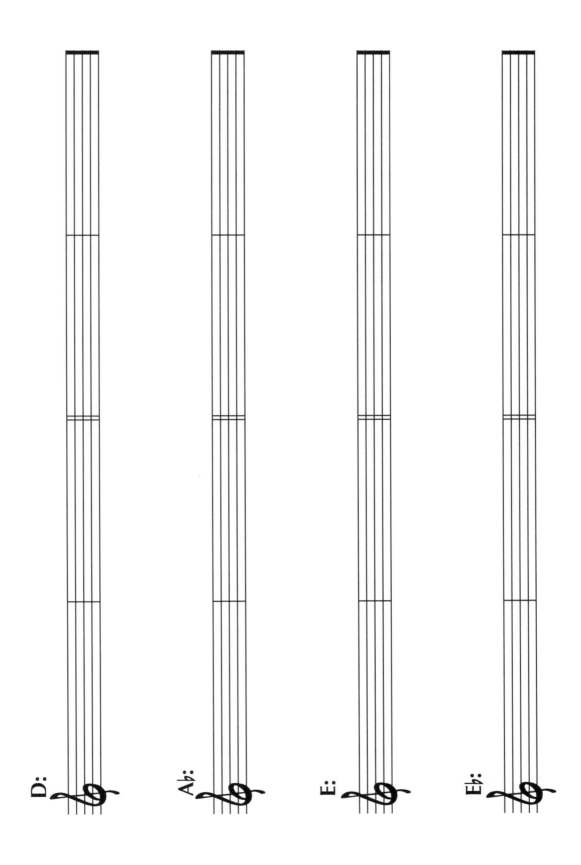

Open Voicings

The term *open*, when referring to a voicing, simply means that the voicing spans an interval greater than an octave. Open voicings are identified as drop-2, drop-3 and drop-2/4.

Drop-2

A drop-2 voicing is created by simply dropping the second highest voice of a four-way close tertian structure down an octave to the bottom of the chord. It is by far the most frequently used open position. This type of voicing allows the listener to hear the individual voices move much more clearly than in a close voicing. It also is used when the melody is pitched relatively high because it supplies the lower instruments with more comfortable notes to play. When harmonizing a melody with substantial leaps, it is a good idea to alternate between open and close voicings.

This next example illustrates the simple process of converting a four way close voicing into drop-2:

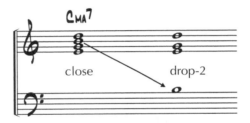

Example 6.15

Notice that the outer voices form a tenth. Because the outer voices are so prevalent in an open voicing, they should form a consonant interval. This can affect chord tone substitution choices, as is seen in the next example.

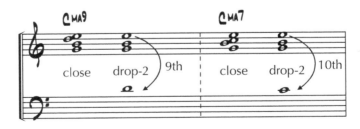

Example 6.16

In the first measure, a ninth has been substituted for the root, and it is the second voice from the top. When that voice is dropped, a ninth interval is formed between the outer voices, which sounds awkward. The second measure corrects the problem by using the root of the chord, thereby creating a tenth in the outer voices when it is dropped down the octave. Play this example on the piano to hear the difference.

When moving from chord to chord with drop-2 voicings, the voices move as they would in four-way close. The only difference is that the individual voices are in different places. Example 6.17 below illustrates the ii–V–I progression in both major and minor keys using drop-2 voicings. The notes are identical to those used in example 6.9, where four-way close ii–V–Is are presented. Notice that you can hear the individual lines more clearly when the progression is in drop-2. Unlike with tonic chords, the outer voices may form dissonant intervals, as unstable chords move from one to another. The ninth interval (D and C) between the outer voices in the D half-diminished chord resolves nicely to an augmented second in the G7, which sounds like a major third (E♭ to B). Play these on the piano and transpose them to all keys as you did with the four-way close progressions.

Example 6.17

The following example offers an interesting contrast to example 6.14 in which the bridge chords of "Sabrosa" are rendered using four-way close voicings. In the following example, the same chords are voiced in drop-2 with the same melody notes (minus the passing tones) on top of each chord. Listen to the audio tracks for each example and you should notice now much more easily you hear the lines move. The examples are played on piano and bass; it would be even clearer with individual horns playing these parts.

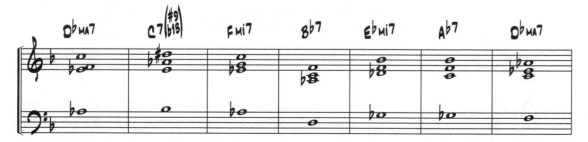

Example 6.18

Drop-3 and Drop-2/4

Drop-3 voicings are also possible. Although used less frequently than drop-2, they can be useful because they also spread out a tertian structure. As the name implies, the third note from the top is dropped an octave. Drop-2/4 involves dropping the second and fourth voices down an octave. In the next two chapters we will see that it makes more sense to think of drop-2/4 voicings as quartal and slash chords.

For most arrangers, and especially for those just learning the craft, four-way close and drop-2 will make up the bulk of your voicings. However, there are other methods that can provide colorful alternatives to your arrangements. These are described in the next two chapters.

Chapter Summary

1. In a four-way close voicing, the four chord tones do not exceed the interval of an octave.

2. In an open position voicing, the chord spans an interval greater than an octave.

3. The root, third, fifth, and seventh can be replaced by chord tones that provide additional tonal colors. These substitutions are dependent upon the chord quality, the key of the moment, and the level of dissonance or consonance desired.

4. A and B chord positions provide the best voice leading and alternate in circle progressions.

5. Only the seventh resolves in major ii–V movement.

6. To convert a close position voicing to a drop-2 voicing, move the second-highest note down to the bottom of the chord.

7. Open voicings also include drop-3 and drop-2/4.

Assignment 6.5

Drop-2 Voicings

Using four-way close voicings, add the three lower notes to the melody line found on the next page according to each chord symbol and chord function. Next, convert the voicing to drop-2 in the grand staff. Use SATB stem directions so that each voice may be easily distinguished. The first chord of each example is provided.

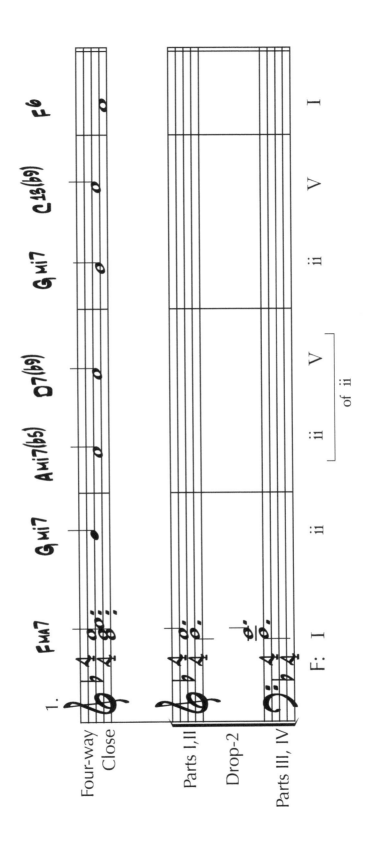

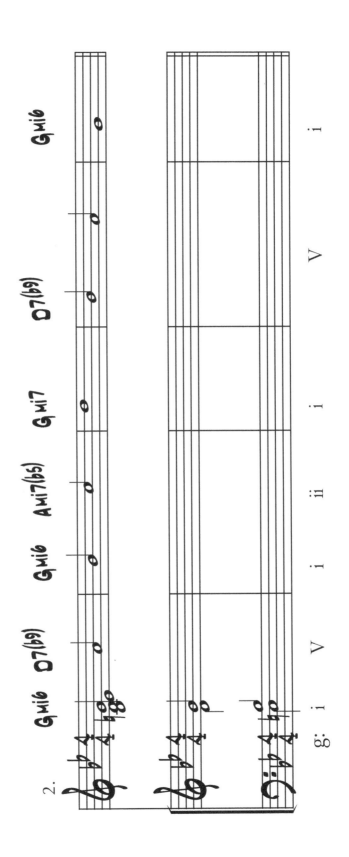

Quartal Harmony

Tertian harmony, as we saw in the preceding chapter, refers to building chords by stacking in thirds. While this is the most common method of building chords, it is not the only way. Arrangers, composers, and theorists have conceived of other systems such as secundal harmony (based upon seconds), quartal harmony (built upon fourths), and quintal harmony (based upon fifths). The use of fourths in jazz became prevalent during the 1960s in the music of artists such as McCoy Tyner, Miles Davis, Joe Henderson and many others. You'll find that if you apply quartal harmony properly, your music will take on a more spacious, hip sound. As we explore quartal harmony in this chapter, we'll build on the concepts introduced in the previous chapter—especially the concept of open voicing structures.

Quartal voicings are constructed with perfect fourths, except in the case of the dominant seventh in which the bottom interval is a tritone. A pianist will usually play this structure with five notes, but in the case of a four-horn ensemble either the top or bottom notes can be eliminated to form a four-note voicing. There are a couple of interesting points about quartal harmony which we will discuss shortly:

1. Quartal voicings can be thought of as drop-2/4 open voicings derived from a ter-

tian structure.

2. Depending on what the root is, the same stack of fourths can form several different chords.

Quartal Harmony = Drop-2/4

As mentioned above, drop-2/4 voicings can be viewed as quartal voicings. This way of thinking about a drop-2/4 voicing is actually simpler than thinking about lowering the second and fourth notes from the top of a chord. This conversion from close position to drop-2/4 is shown in the example below.

The first chord in example 7.1 is a five-note C major chord structure that contains the root, sixth, fifth, third, and ninth. It is in close position (i.e., it does not exceed an interval of an octave). The second chord has the same notes as the first but is voiced with a drop-2/4 voicing. The second and fourth notes from the top (the A and the E) have been dropped an octave resulting in a chord built entirely of stacked perfect fourths.

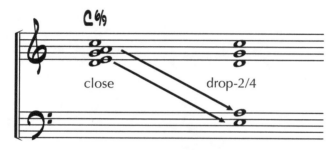

Example 7.1

Latin Roots

Many of the terms related to musical intervals come from Latin root words. Let's take them in order: the word *unison* comes from two Latin roots. *Uni-* is a prefix that means "one," and *sonus* means "sound." So literally, *unison* means "one sound." The word *secundal* comes from the Latin word *secundus* which means "second" (as in first, second, third). So *secundal* means "second-oriented." The word *tertian* comes from the Latin word *tertius* which means "third." So *tertian* means "third-oriented." The word *quartal* comes from the Latin word *quartus* which means "fourth." So *quartal* means "fourth-oriented." And lastly, the word *quintal* comes from the Latin word *quintus* which means "fifth." So *quintal* means "fifth-oriented."

Transposing Quartal Voicings

The same quartal voicing can be used to express several different chords, as is demonstrated in the next example. The chord labeled as a C6/9 contains the root, fifth, ninth, sixth, and third of the chord. These same notes can form several other chords, such as an Fma13 and an Ami11. Since these are five-note structures, the substitution chart discussed in the previous chapter doesn't apply quite the same way. With five-note chords, is it possible to have thirteenths with fifths, elevenths with fifths, and roots with ninths in the same chord. Understanding what chord tone you want for the top of the voicing (especially when voicing the melody) is critical here. As shown below in example 7.2, the top chord tone of the voicing when interpreted as a C6/9 is the root; the top note is the fifth of the Fma13; it is the third of the Amin11. In each case the notes are identical. The chord tones are listed in the boxes to the right of each chord. Quartal voicings are very versatile and flexible, adding another dimension to your voicing choices.

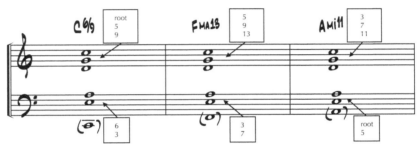

Example 7.2

The arrangements used in this text are scored for four horns, and you'll see that quartal voicings are used for scoring the four parts in various places. As we will see below, adapting these five-note quartal voicings to work as four-note structures is a simple process.

Quartal Voicings as Four-Note Structures

As we observed in example 7.1, quartal voicings are considered "open" because they exceed the distance of an octave. By omitting either the top or bottom note, the remaining stack of fourths still exceeds an octave; there is just one less fourth interval than was illustrated in the examples 7.1 and 7.2. The next example (7.3) revisits the second measure of the open voicing ii–V–I seen in example 6.17, but in this case the tonic chord (i.e., the I) is voiced as a quartal voicing. You will see and hear that these structures can be used effectively in a four-voice context.

The arrows in example 7.3 illustrate the additional voice motion resulting from the quartal tonic chord (the C6/9). The B (the third of the G7) moves down to the A (the sixth of the C6/9) in the second measure, however in the first measure of the example, the B of the G7 remains as the seventh of the Cma7. Inner voice motion helps define the progression and leads the listener's ear through the chords. As you hear the audio track (which also includes chord roots not pictured here) observe the difference between the warmth of the Cma7 in the first measure and the more spacious sound of the C6/9.

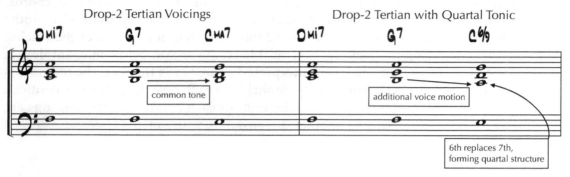

Example 7.3

Quartal Voicings as Dominants

So far we have only discussed major and minor quartal voicings. It is possible to use quartal voicings for dominant chords as well, but in order to do so the bottom interval of the voicing must be altered. By changing the bottom interval into a tritone (diminished fifth or augmented fourth) the chord becomes a bright-sounding dominant seventh.

The following example illustrates the conversion of major quartal structures into dominant quartal structures.

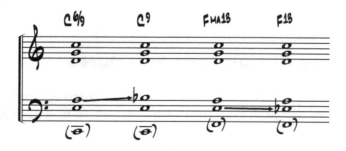

Example 7.4

We have seen in example 7.2 that a single quartal voicing can support a variety of roots. In example 7.4 the first and third chords contain the same tones above two different roots, forming a C6/9 and an Fma13. Converting the C6/9 chord into a C9 chord is accomplished by raising the sixth (the A) to a B♭—the seventh of the dominant chord. Converting the Fma13 chord into a dominant quality chord—an F13—is accomplished by lowering the seventh (the E) to an E♭, which is the seventh of the dominant chord.

Seeing and hearing these specialized voicings in context reveals the hip, open sound that they provide for an arrangement. Let's take a look at a chord progression that uses quartal harmony.

Example 7.5

Notice how this example demonstrates several chord structures: a major thirteenth with the fifth as the top note of the voicing (the Cma13), two major 6/9s with the root as the top note of the voicing (the F6/9 and C6/9), and a dominant quartal chord (the G9). Quartal voicings offer additional options for arrangers beyond tertian harmony, providing a different way to use open voicing structures.

"So What" Voicings

This voicing, named for Miles Davis' famous modal composition, is similar to the quartal voicings discussed above, but this structure is brightened by the presence of a major third interval on top of the chord. This voicing has the same properties as the quartal chords—it is a drop-2/4 voicing and is transposable.

This next example illustrates the conversion from close to drop-2/4 open position. It is the same process illustrated in example 7.1, but in this case the first chord is a Cma13 rather than a C6/9. The first chord is a five-note chord structure that contains the seventh, the thirteenth, the fifth, the third, and the ninth. Notice that in this chord, the seventh, thirteenth, and fifth are adjacent to one another, forming a colorful, dissonant cluster. This chord, unlike the C6/9 shown in example 7.1, has a major seventh. Therefore, when you drop the thirteenth (the A) down an octave, that leaves the G and B as a bright-sounding major third on top of the voicing. Also, as we saw with quartal chords, this same group of notes could also form other chords if you simply changed the bass note.

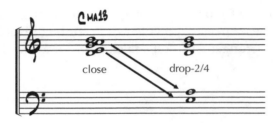

Example 7.6

Transposing "So What" Voicings

"So What" voicings have two important characteristics: they have a bright, modern sound, and they are easily transposable. As is the case with quartal voicings, "So What" voicings can also have several possible roots, creating different major and minor chords. The most common uses of this structure are to create major thirteenth chords and minor eleventh chords, but composers also use them for major ♯11 and suspended chords as well.

The next example contains a single "So What" structure notated four times, each with a different bass note.

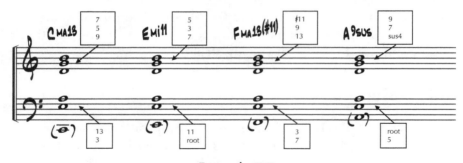

Example 7.7

"So What" and Quartal Voicings in Context

Quartal and "So What" structures provide new color choices for the arranger. On the following page is a progression in which these voicings are combined:

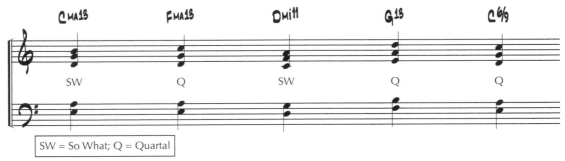

Example 7.8

Notice the smooth voicing leading between chords in the above example. Although these hip, edgy voicings may be just what you are looking for in some situations, they should probably not be your primary choice. Tertian harmony is still the "meat and potatoes" of the arranger's voicing choices.

Chapter Summary

1. Quartal chords are built entirely of fourths.
2. Quartal chords can be viewed as drop-2/4 tertian voicings.
3. Quartal chords are transposable.
4. Dominants can be formed by changing the bottom interval of a quartal chord to a tritone.
5. "So What" chords are quartal chords brightened by a major third on top.
6. "So What" chords are transposable.

Assignment 7.1

Quartal Chords

In the staff provided on the next page, notate the five-note quartal voicings under the given notes. The voicing type is listed for each chord. Put three notes in the treble clef staff and two notes in the bass clef staff. The first chord is provided.

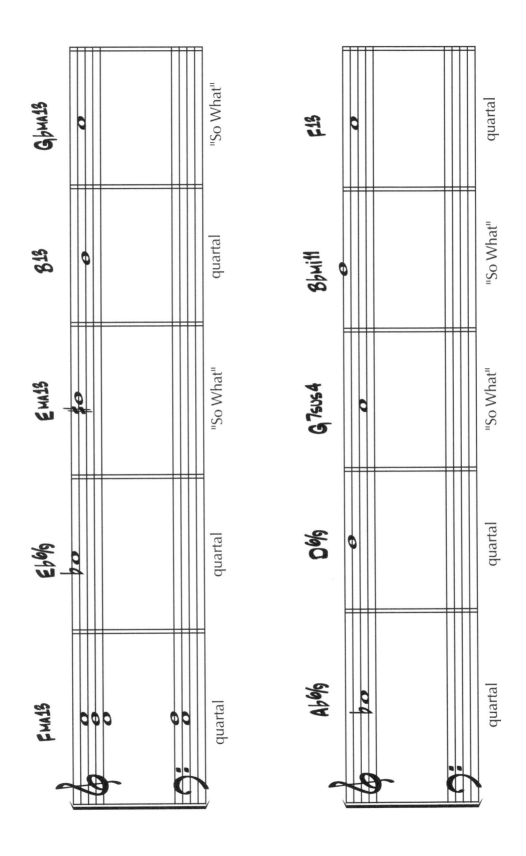

Slash Chords

A slash chord is a symbol that indicates a bass note other than the normal root of the chord. For instance, in the example shown below, the Cma7 chord should be played over a D bass note. This chord symbol would be pronounced "C major seven over D."

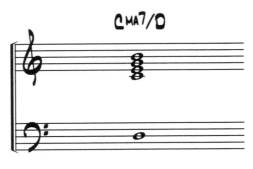

Example 8.1

If you page through a fake book, you'll see plenty of examples of slash chord notation. Gaining an understanding of how the notation functions adds a useful tool to your collection of voicing possibilities.

Uses of Slash Chords

There are three primary reasons why jazz musicians use slash chords: to improve bass lines, to notate an exact sound, and to simplify complex structures.

Smoothing Out Bass Lines

Bass players are trained to play roots of chords when reading a lead sheet, along with the various passing tones heard in walking bass lines. As a result of playing chord roots, a bass line can include rather wide leaps. Slash chord symbols smooth out a bass line by indicating chord inversions. For instance, the example shown below is a C triad in first inversion.

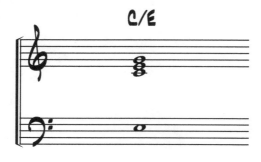

Example 8.2

With this simple method at the writer's disposal, it's easy to smooth out the bass line as chords progress from one to the next.

The last eight bars of the famous Duke Ellington standard "In A Mellow Tone" will serve to illustrate this point. It starts on the Dbma7 which functions as the IV chord.

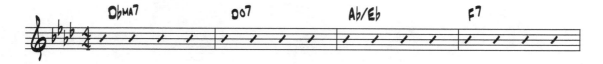

Example 8.3

In this progression, the Ab chord was given an Eb as the bass note (second inversion) to create a smooth line for the bass player to play. Notice how the bass line moves up in a stepwise fashion from Db to D to Eb and then to F.

Notating An Exact Sound

Another reason why slash chords are so useful for composers and arrangers is that they communicate a high degree of specificity. By using slash chords, composers and arrangers can dictate to the rhythm section an exact chord sound that includes certain notes while omitting others. Let's say, for instance, that you want the rhythm section to play a Cma7(♯5) chord but without playing the ninth. Many pianists would consider playing the ninth of the chord since it's such a common substitution. But with a slash chord, E/C (pronounced "E over C"), you could quickly and easily show exactly what notes you want played. When the rhythm section members react to that chord symbol, they would play C in the bass, and E, G♯ and B—the notes of an E triad—above it. This leaves out the unwanted D.

Simplifying Complex Structures

One of the most important reasons for using slash chords is that they can express complex chord structures in a simplified manner. Suspended chords offer a useful and common example. While this chord is often indicated with the "sus" designation, as in C7sus, slash chord notation is often used instead, as in B♭/C. The B♭ triad includes a B♭, D, and F. With a C bass note, these tones form the seventh (the B♭), 9th (the D), and the suspended 4th (the F) of a C7sus. Therefore, colorful tones (especially the ninth) are added to the chord and the arranger need only think of the notes of a B♭ triad. The following illustrates this extremely common chord with the chord tones indicated in the boxes.

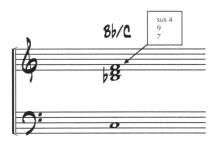

Example 8.4

Chord Over Chord

Most of the time when you see a slash chord it indicates a chord over a bass note like the ones shown above. But sometimes the part of the chord below the slash is not just a bass note, but a full chord. This "chord over chord" type of symbol is called a *polychord*. When a slash chord indicates a polychord, the part of the symbol below the slash will have a chord quality written next to it such as "triad," "7," or "ma7."

Having the ability to notate one chord stacked on top of another chord can be a very useful tool for an arranger to have in his or her toolbox. This is especially true when dealing with dominant chords. Dominant seventh chords can be quite elaborate, but utilizing a slash chord symbol can make it much easier to notate a complex chord. When using this type of chord notation, the bottom symbol will normally indicate a letter followed by the numeral "7." This serves as the foundation of the chord. The upper symbol is a triad that provides interesting and useful chord tone substitutions. Providing harmonic color for dominant seventh chord structures is a very important part of jazz theory. As with the suspended chords we examined above, it is helpful to have a simple way to express a complex structure.

Important!

In a "chord over bass note" slash chord, the bottom letter will not have a chord quality next to it—it will just be a letter. But if the letter below the slash has a chord quality written next to it, you can be sure that the chord symbol is a "chord over chord" or polychord.

For example, a C7(♯9)(♭13) chord looks like a complicated symbol, and it is. Fortunately, that same chord can also be notated as an A♭/C7. Not only will the proper notes be played, it will also be properly voiced as well. Other common examples are A/C7 which is a slash chord version of C13(♭9) and D/C7 which is a C13(♯11). The following example demonstrates these chord constructions.

Example 8.5

The example above shows the slash chord symbol between the staves and the more complicated single symbol above the treble staff. The chord tones supplied by the upper triad symbol are listed in the boxes to the right of the chord symbol. Like the quartal and "So What" voicings, the A♭/C7 and D/C7 slash chords are five-note structures (not including the root). The A/C7 is a four-note chord also (not including the root). Notice that the enharmonic spelling is flexible when using these voicings. In the A♭/C7, the E♭ in the treble staff appears to be a minor third, but since there is a major third in the chord (in the bass clef), it is an enharmonically misspelled raised ninth (D♯). The reason for the E♭ rather than a D♯ is that the upper triad is an A♭ chord, which of course contains an E♭. It would look pretty odd with a D♯, and it would not serve the purpose of simplifying the chord.

Notice also that the upper triad is in second inversion. By using this particular inversion, the resulting structure is in drop-2/4 for the A♭/C7 and D/C7 and in drop-2 for the A/C7. The next example illustrates this with the same process as seen with quartal and "So What" voicings.

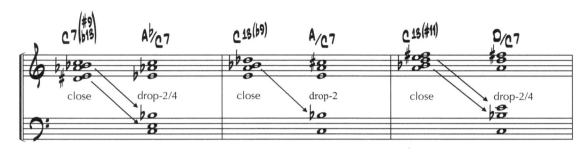

Example 8.6

The close position voicing in example 8.6 is notated correctly as far as note names are concerned. The slash chord version, in open position, contains the "incorrect" but more easily read enharmonic alterations.

We will discuss slash chords in context in subsequent chapters when we examine the example tunes. Before we get to those later chapters, let's look at a short example from one of the example tunes.

Example 8.7

The major seventh chords are voiced with "So What" voicings in which the seventh is in the melody. The dominant thirteenth chords are bright ♯11 slash chords. It is interesting to see how smoothly the voice leading works. The upper part of the "So What" chords are all common to the subsequent upper part of the slash chord.

We'll be revisiting slash chords in chapter 13, "Three-Part Writing." In that chapter we'll see that the upper triad can be voiced by a three-horn section (as was done, for example, by Art Blakey and the Jazz Messengers). The upper triad of a slash chord can also be scored for a single section in a big band or by a pianist who often will play the top chord in the right hand and the bottom one in the left hand.

Voicing Summary

This unit contains information about tertian, quartal, "So What," and slash chord voicings. You should base most of your thinking on tertian harmony because building chords in thirds is the foundation of our harmonic system. Furthermore, we found that the more specialized voicings presented above (i.e., quartal, "So What" and slash chords) may all be viewed as tertian drop-2 and drop-2/4 voicings.

Although we've discussed several voicing techniques, arrangers normally use the same voicing type throughout a phrase or section so that the voices move smoothly. This is particularly true when harmonizing a stepwise melody. However, moving from one technique to another is very common and effective—particularly when the range of the melody changes or unwanted repeated notes are found in the lower voices. Remember that you are writing individual melodies for each horn or voice as the harmony progresses.

Thus far we have discussed the harmonization of chord tones. Not every tone is a chord tone, of course. Learning how these non-chord tones are harmonized is an important part of the journey toward becoming a successful jazz arranger. This process is explained in the next chapter.

Chapter Summary

1. Slash chords are used in jazz standards to notate inversions that create smoother bass lines.
2. Slash chords allow you to notate an exact chord sound.
3. Slash chords allow you to simplify complex chord symbols.
4. If the bottom chord does not have a quality next to it, it means chord over bass note.
5. If the bottom chord has a quality next to it, it means chord over chord.

Assignment 8.1

Slash Chords

On the next page, notate slash chords according to the directions listed below. The first chord has been completed for you.

- If the chord is a dominant 7(♯9)(♭13), put the upper triad in second inversion and add the seventh and third in the bass clef (seventh on top).

- If the chord is a dominant 13(♯11), put the upper triad in second inversion, and add the third and seventh in the bass clef (third on top).

- If the chord is a dominant 13(♭9), put the upper triad in second inversion and the seventh in the bass clef.

- If the chord is a dominant 7sus, put the upper triad in root position and the root of the chord name in the bass clef.

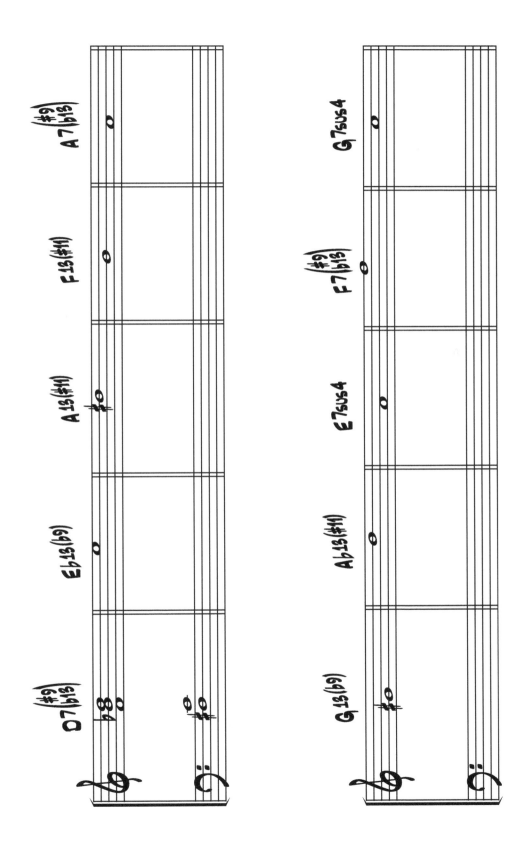

Nonharmonic Tones

Traditional music theory books invariably contain a chapter devoted to tones that fall between the harmonic cracks—the "nonharmonic" tones. These important notes often provide the color and spice that make a piece of music unique. Fortunately, these tones are not difficult to understand. In this chapter we will be focusing on the following:

Passing tones: Tones that pass by step between two different chord tones.

Neighboring tones: Tones that move away from and back to the same pitch in a stepwise fashion.

Double Neighboring Tones: Two tones that move as their name implies, surrounding a harmonic tone, either diatonically or chromatically. Often the upper neighboring tone is diatonic and the lower is chromatic. This is a very common melodic technique used by jazz composers and improvisers. Double neighboring tones are also referred to as *enclosures*.

The Bach-like example below illustrates these three nonharmonic tones.

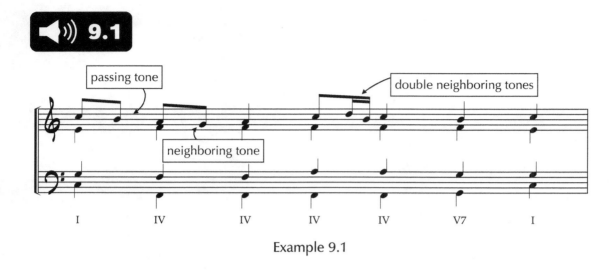

Example 9.1

In the example shown above, the soprano voice contains three nonharmonic tones. The B is a passing tone moving between C and A. The G is a neighboring tone moving from the A and then back up to the same A. The D and B sixteenth notes are double neighboring tones surrounding the subsequent C.

There are other types of nonharmonic tones, but in this book we will be focusing mainly on passing tones and neighboring tones. However, to gain a more thorough understanding of nonharmonic tones, I would suggest that you consult a traditional music theory book on this subject.

What is a Nonharmonic Tone in a Jazz Context?

Before we begin our discussion of nonharmonic tones, we must ask an important question: How can you identify which notes are chord tones and which are not, particularly in the rich harmonic environment of jazz?

In the jazz idiom, many tones can be considered chord tones. For example, an F can be the root of an F chord but also the thirteenth of an Ab chord and the flat fifth of a B chord. So under what circumstances will that same F be considered a nonharmonic tone? The answer lies in the harmonic context of the music at that particular time. As long as you know how each chord is functioning, and if you understand the available substitutions for the various chord tones (see example 6.3) you will be able to identify a tone as either a chord tone or as a nonharmonic tone. Often they are the second, fourth, or sixth above a chord root; in other words, the notes in between the fundamental tones of root, third, fifth, and seventh. But harmonic context is the governing factor most of the time.

Texture

The discussion that follows will involve working in a homophonic texture (i.e., a texture in which the melody is on top and the accompanying parts move in the same direction and with the same rhythm as the melody). As the lines that are scored under a melody follow its contour, the nonharmonic tones in the melody must be treated in some way if the texture is to remain homophonic. When harmonizing any melody the arranger must take into account multiple considerations. The arranger must think in a horizontal fashion in order to make the lower parts natural-sounding and easy to play. Simultaneously, the arranger must think in a vertical fashion, taking into account the harmonic context.

Approach Techniques

The term *approach* is often used to describe how the individual parts lead toward a harmonic goal. There are four types of approaches described below:

1. Diatonic
2. Diminished
3. Dominant and secondary dominant (with or without the related ii chord)
4. Parallel (both chromatic and nonchromatic)

The following examples illustrate these techniques in detail. Most of the examples involve a stepwise melody. In each case, the melody must be analyzed to see which tones are harmonic and which are nonharmonic. Observe (and play if you want) the lower voices and how they move; they are easy to follow because the stem directions, written in SATB format, help to identify each line. The goal is to write lower parts that have a musical flow. In these examples, each approach technique is labeled. Accidentals carry through the entirety of each example.

Diatonic Approach

The melody in the following example is simply a C major scale, and the chord used to harmonize this passage is, naturally, a C major chord. So the chord tones are C, E, and G. When using the diatonic approach technique labeled with a D, the nonharmonic tones are scored using the notes of the governing key. This is also referred to as *diatonic planing* as each voice moves in parallel motion with the melody.

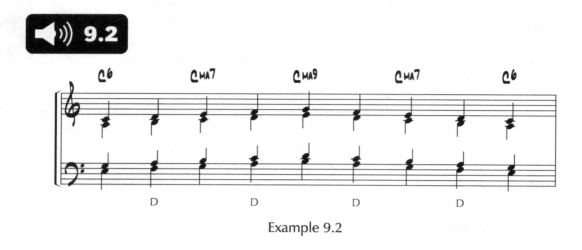

Example 9.2

Notice that each voice simply moves up and down the scale and the chord tones take turns being the root, third, and fifth of the fundamental C chord. When the root is the melody tone, the chord is a C6; when the third is the melody, the chord contains a seventh; and when the fifth is the melodic tone, the chord contains a ninth. These chord tones come about because of the lines created by the inner voices.

Diminished Seventh Approach

The diminished seventh approach technique (abbreviated "Dim") tonicizes different harmonic tones. These tones are temporarily heard as brief "tonics" as the unstable diminished seventh chords resolve. In this example, the voice leading of each line creates a C6 for each harmonic tone. Also note that the diminished chords are constructed with the same four notes—B, D, F, and A♭ (or G♯ depending on the direction of the line).

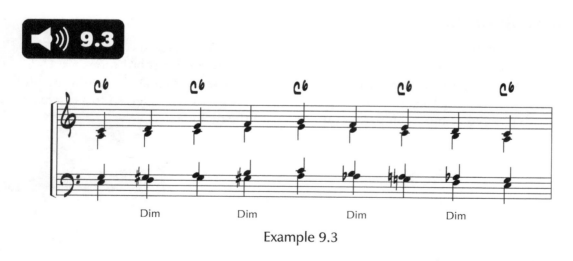

Example 9.3

The next example illustrates the same diminished seventh approach technique, but this time in a minor key. The diminished chord used for the nonharmonic tones is the same. The C chord is the same too, except that it has a minor third.

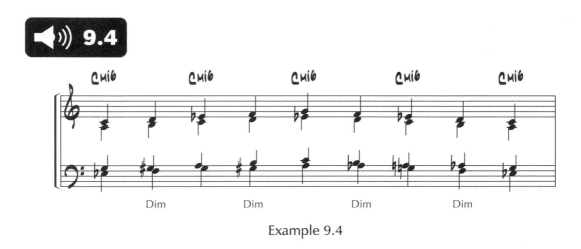

Example 9.4

Diminished Seventh Chords

Diminished seventh chords are symmetrical chords built entirely with minor thirds. Therefore, a C diminished seventh chord, E♭ diminished seventh chord, F♯ diminished seventh chord, and A diminished seventh chord are all formed using these same four notes. The same thing is true for C♯, E, G, and B♭, and also for D, F, A♭, and B. Therefore, there are really only three unique diminished seventh chords.

Dominant and Secondary Dominant Approach (with Preceding ii)

Secondary dominants with or without a preceding ii chord can also be used with nonharmonic tones. In this method, secondary dominants are constructed under nonharmonic tones prior to chord tones in the melody. This is somewhat similar to the diminished seventh approach method discussed above. The example on the following page illustrates this method.

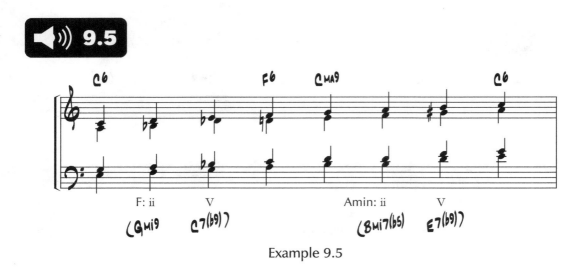

Example 9.5

As you listen to the audio recording of the above example, you may notice a particularly disjunct line. The alto part has two awkward intervals: the minor third between the Bb and Db, and the augmented second between the F and G♯. Therefore this technique may not be the best solution for this particular melody.

Composers, arrangers, and jazz performers frequently utilize double neighboring tone motion to surround "target" notes. Using the dominant of the key as well as secondary dominant approaches (often including the related ii chord as seen in the previous example) can provide a good solution when harmonizing double neighboring tones. Our next example illustrates this process in two locations.

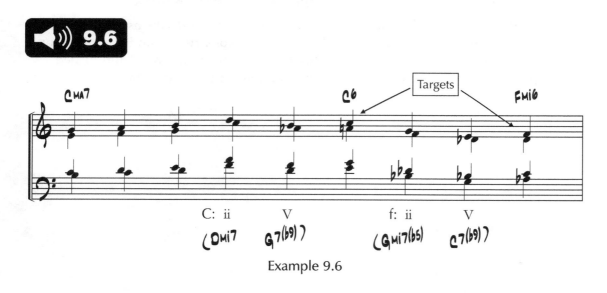

Example 9.6

The melody in example 9.6 is in C major, but it includes two double neighboring motions: the D and B surround the target note C, and the G and E surround the target note F, harmonized with an Fmin6 chord. Both sets of double neighboring tones are harmonized with ii–V motion and these chord symbols are indicated below the staff in parentheses. This works well because the melodic line and inner voices are driven forward by the harmonic motion provided by the ii–Vs.

Parallel Approaches

The previous examples illustrate techniques that utilize harmonic context. Parallel approach techniques, however, are essentially nonfunctional.

The first type of parallel approach we will examine is the chromatic parallel approach. Chromatic melodies are relatively simple to harmonize. After determining which tones of a melody are the harmonic tones, *harmonize these first*. The lower parts supporting these target tones are then simply approached chromatically in the same direction as the melody. This is also known as *chromatic planing*. The abbreviation for this technique is CP.

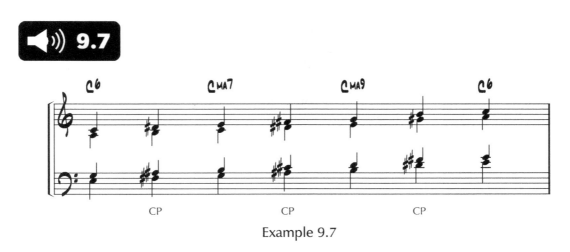

Example 9.7

Another type of parallel approach is the nonchromatic parallel approach. This is another nonfunctional technique in which the lower tones move parallel to the melody, as in the chromatic approach. Each voice moves the same exact distance as the melody, as well as in the same direction. The abbreviation is NCP as in "nonchromatic parallel."

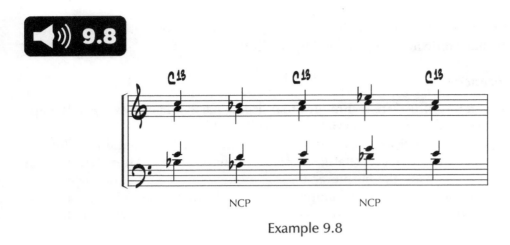

Example 9.8

These techniques look relatively simple when harmonizing basic melodies. By examining excerpts from the example tunes, however, we can view these techniques in more realistic situations. The examples will illustrate that choosing one technique over another is an important decision, especially when trying to write lower parts that are natural-sounding. One of the most common problems that arrangers face is the writing of awkward repeated notes in accompanying voices. While this is sometimes unavoidable, arrangers should do their best to limit them, especially in eighth or sixteenth note lines.

Approach Techniques in Context

Now that we have covered the basics, let's see how these concepts work in the context of actual arrangements. The examples below are scored with four-note chords in the traditional SATB format using four-way close voicings. The principles outlined here are equally valid when scoring with open voicings.

Additionally, these solutions may or may not be seen again in the specifically arranged versions of the example tunes in upcoming chapters. These arrangements will be presented in a variety of ways that include unison writing, countermelodies, and harmonized sections. Because we are currently exploring the scoring of nonharmonic tones, homophonic textures predominate in these examples.

"Why Not Now"

The bridge of the example tune "Why Not Now" offers us a good opportunity to view various techniques because of its stepwise nature, its simple harmonic function, and the variety of half step and whole step motion. The example shown below contains the final four measures of the melody with the nonharmonic tones labeled. The abbreviation *PT* stands for "passing tone" and *NT* stands for "neighboring tone."

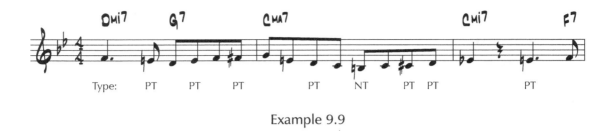

Example 9.9

The next example illustrates both diatonic and chromatic parallel approaches. Notice that the half step motion in the melody is harmonized with a chromatically parallel solution in the lower voices. This version works well, but it is very consonant or "inside" harmonically. The abbreviation *D* stands for "diatonic" and *CP* stands for "chromatic parallel."

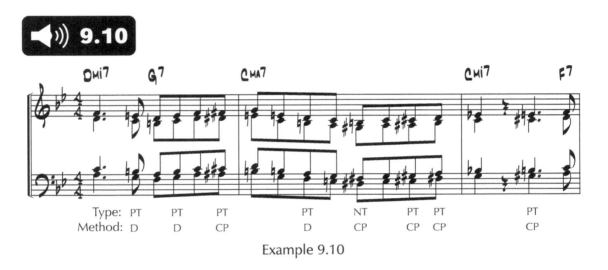

Example 9.10

The next example adds the diminished seventh chord approach technique to the same excerpt but retains some of the chromatic approaches. Here the diminished chords serve to tonicize the chord tones, giving the line more emphasis as it moves forward. The abbreviation *Dim* stands for "diminished."

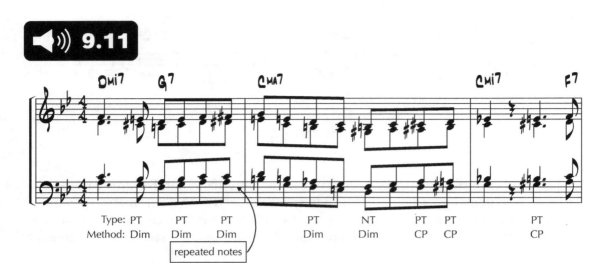

Example 9.11

The version illustrated in the above example would work just fine except for the repeated notes (C and A) in the bottom voices in the last two notes of the first measure. It would therefore be best to use the chromatic parallel harmonization in that location as shown in example 9.10. However, as you listen to the example, notice that the resolution of the diminished sevenths seems to drive the melody forward with a sense of urgency.

This next example demonstrates dominant ii–V function. This version begins with smooth diatonic motion in the first measure in which the Dmi7 (the ii) and G7 (the V) occur, and includes another ii–V in the key of C harmonized under the second and third melodic tones in the second measure.

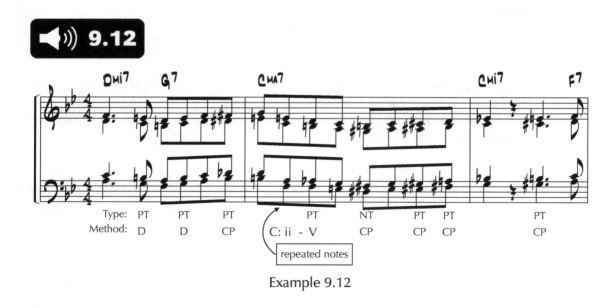

Example 9.12

The excerpt in the example shown above would certainly work, but once again there are repeated notes (F)—this time only in the bottom voice. The arranger should find another solution in order to avoid the uncomfortable repeated notes.

"Sabrosa"

In the next few examples we will discuss various approach techniques using a fragment of the bridge from "Sabrosa." This short fragment contains only two nonharmonic tones: the passing tone G and the neighboring tone E.

Example 9.13

In the example shown below, diminished sevenths are used to harmonize both of the nonharmonic tones. Notice it's the same diminished chord for both tones.

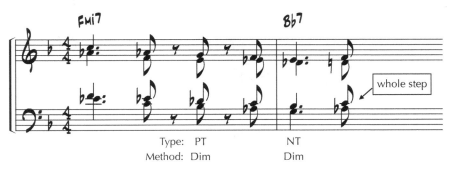

Example 9.14

The E on beat one of the second bar may be better harmonized with a chromatic approach because the tenor line (the B♭ to C) is a whole step while all the other voices move by half step.

In the next example, the E in the second bar is harmonized with a chromatic approach instead of the diminished seventh approach shown in the last example. The difference is slight, but it is smoother because all the voices are moving chromatically.

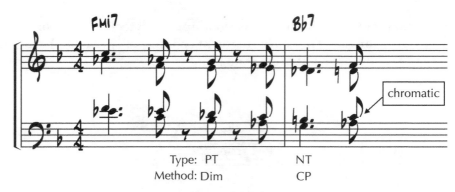

Example 9.15

"December Serenade"

The opening melody in "December Serenade" offers the opportunity to employ several techniques. The line includes passing tones that move through the melody both by whole and half step. The melody is sequential, so it makes sense to duplicate the technique as each two-measure motive is restated down in whole steps.

Example 9.16

There is a simple way to handle this excerpt. The first passing tone in each sequential statement (i.e., measures 1, 3, and 5) is best harmonized diatonically using the "key of the moment" which is F major in measure 1, E♭ major in measure 3, and D♭ major in measure 5. The other passing tone moves chromatically, so chromatic approaches are used for each sequence. In measure 5, there is a whole step motion (the F to E♭) leading to the Ema7(♭5). A parallel approach is used here (the nonchromatic variety) and the voicing is reduced to three notes from here to the end because of the low range of the melody. The final nonharmonic tone (in the last measure) moves chromatically, from D♭ to C, so a chromatic parallel approach is used. Listen for the difference among the diatonic and parallel approaches, both chromatic and nonchromatic. Let's see how that would look:

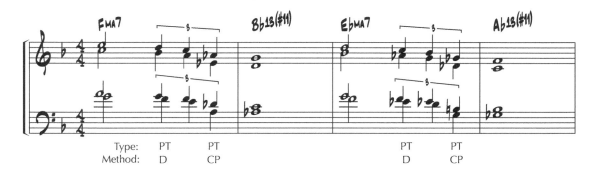

Example 9.17

Chapter Summary

1. Passing tones, neighboring tones, and double neighboring tones are the most common nonharmonic tones.
2. You can identify nonharmonic tones by examining the harmonic context of the passage.
3. Approach techniques:
   (a) Diatonic
   (b) Diminished seventh
   (c) Dominant and secondary dominants (with related ii chord)
   (d) Parallel (both chromatic and nonchromatic)
4. These are used in a homophonic texture in which every note of a melody is harmonized.

Assignment 9.1

Approach Methods

Complete the approach exercises located on the next several pages. Use the appropriate approach technique indicated for each exercise. Nonharmonic tones are indicated with an "X" note head. Use SATB stem directions in four-way close or drop-2 positions as suggested. Read the instructions carefully. Each exercise is started for you.

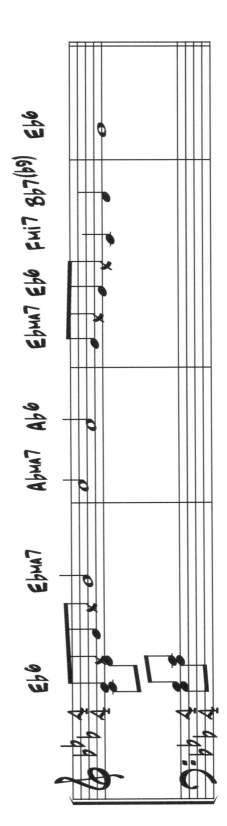

Diatonic Approach

Use four-way close throughout. Hint: there should be no accidentals in this solution until the Bb7(b9).

Diminished Seventh Approach

In this exercise, which of the three diminished sevenths will you choose? Use the one that contains the nonharmonic tone that you are voicing. Use four-way close for measures 1, 3, and 4, and drop-2 in measure 2.

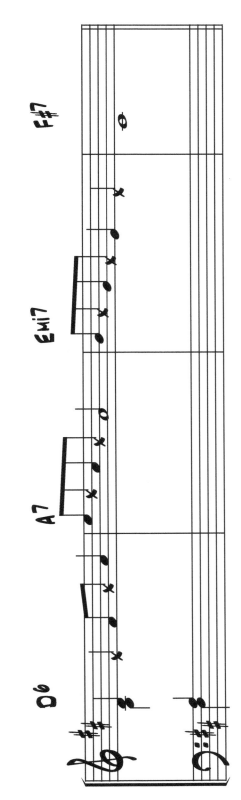

Dominant Approach

The first two notes are given to illustrate that the A♭ neighboring tone is harmonized with notes of a C7 (the V of Fmi7). Take note of the ♭13 (the melodic tone A♭) and the ♭9 (the D♭). These are tones that belong to the "key of the moment" which is F minor. Think about this as you complete the rest of the exercise. Use four-way close throughout.

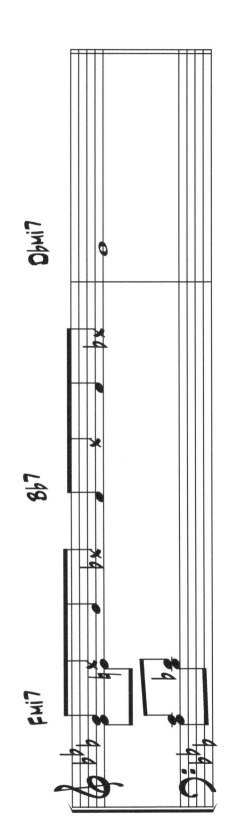

Chromatic Parallel Approach

Use four-way close and drop-2 at your discretion, but consider alternating voicing types as the melody leaps. Hint: Voice the target note first, then move backwards and voice the approaching nonharmonic tone.

Assignment 9.2

Voicing and Approach Summary Project

Arrange the melody on the next page for four voices in a homophonic texture. Pay careful attention to the instructions underneath the grand staff—these instructions identify the voicing methods and approach methods that you must use as you complete the assignment. The instructions given correspond to the symbol key given below:

Symbol Key

Abbreviation	Meaning of Abbreviation
FWC	Four Way Close
D2	Drop-2
Dim	Diminished Seventh Approach
D	Diatonic Approach
CP	Chromatic Parallel Approach
ii–V	ii–V Approach
YD	You Decide!

As you work, be careful of the following issues:

- Use SATB stem directions so that each voice may be easily identified.

- Anticipations: When you see a tied melodic tone on the "and" of four, use the harmony of the chord in the following measure.

- Chord symbols: Some contain the alterations needed while others do not. Consider using sixths rather than sevenths on the i and iv chords.

- Enharmonic spelling: For example, a B♭ melody note may be the raised ninth of a G7 chord.

- Harmonize every note of the melody.

And finally, be sure to listen to the audio track of the music in this assignment:

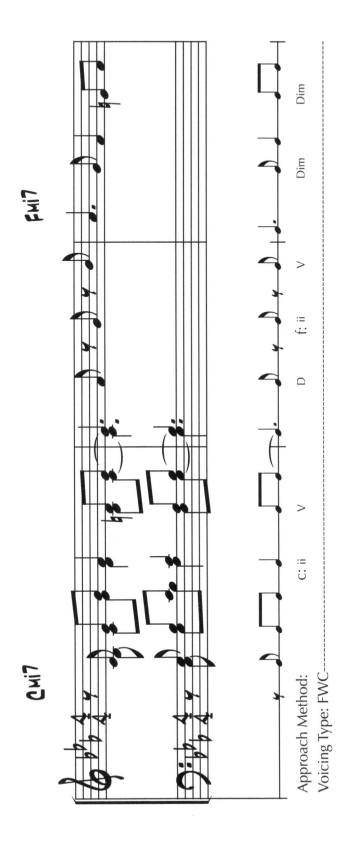

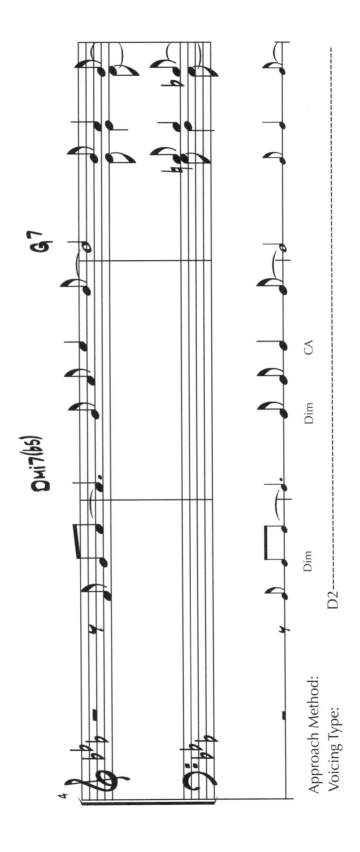

Approach Method:

Voicing Type:

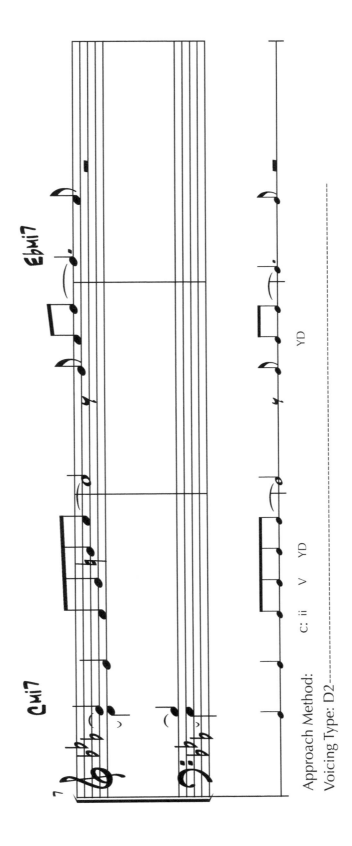

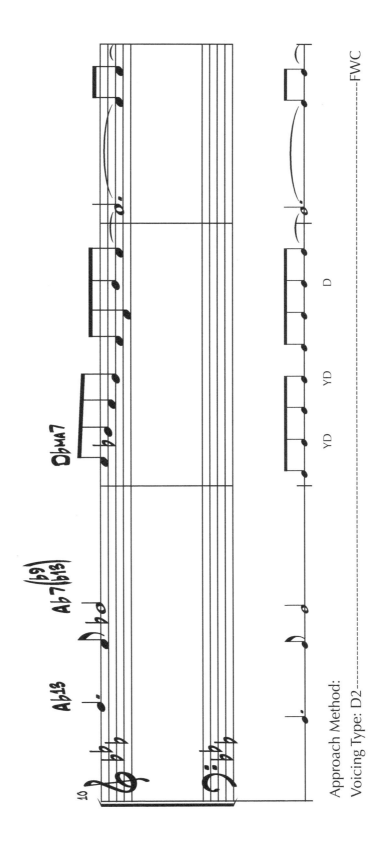

Approach Method:

Voicing Type: D2 ---------------------FWC

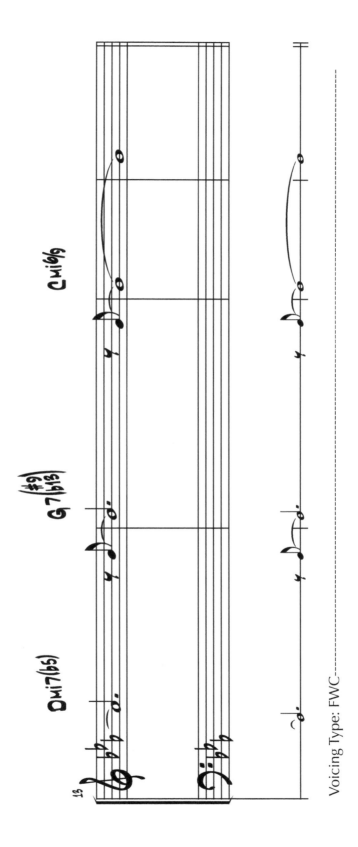

Part IV

Writing An Arrangement

Thus far we have discussed important aspects of form—from the simple song forms that dominate the jazz idiom to common ways in which arrangers manipulate these song forms to create complete arrangements. We have also explored instrumentation and voicing techniques. Now it's time to put that knowledge to use as you begin writing your own arrangements.

Your first task will be to sketch out your first arrangement using a format similar to the schematic diagram assignment in chapter 3. For this arrangement you can use the exercise tunes supplied in appendix A, jazz standards, or an original composition. Initially, we'll only be scoring the melody for two and four horns plus rhythm section.

Once you are comfortable with writing the melody portion (also known as the *head*) of your arrangement, we'll move forward into the additional sections that make an arrangement your own creation. We will explore introductions, endings, solis, shout choruses, interludes, and solo sections with backgrounds. We will then add them to our arrangement. There is a special chapter devoted to problems and potential solutions. If you're having a problem, you may find the solution there.

Planning An Arrangement

When traveling to an unfamiliar destination, you would probably not drive off in your car without a map or at least some idea of where you were going. Likewise, most arrangers shouldn't write an arrangement from beginning to end without first having some concept of the direction and focus of the chart. Previously I have used the term *road map*, a word that implies that a route and final destination were planned from the very beginning. That's what we'll be doing in this chapter—determining where our arrangement will go and the route it will take.

Preliminary Steps: Listening and Analysis

Before any actual writing begins, you will need a foundation upon which to build the plan of the arrangement. It is crucial to understand the tune from every angle and to have a familiarity with other arrangers' work on the same tune. Therefore, analysis and listening are important tasks to undertake when starting an arrangement.

Analyze the Tune

As you make a thorough study of the tune, strive to understand the form, melody, harmony, and the basic rhythmic feel. Play the tune on your instrument and comp the chords on the piano. When I'm familiarizing myself with a tune that I want to arrange, I like to play it on the piano in other keys—this generates ideas that may not have occurred to me in the original key.

Listen to Recordings

Another way to get ideas for your arrangement is to listen to recordings of the tune you wish to arrange. There may be a famous, classic recording of the tune. If this is the case, you at least should be familiar with this recording even if you don't particularly like it. On the other hand, there may be some new version that inspires you. Either way, listening to the ways that other writers have treated the tune will give you some good ideas. While you cannot copy an arrangement note for note, you can emulate the general characteristics. Throughout the history of jazz, composers and arrangers have constantly influenced one another and borrowed each other's material. In this way the genre has been able to develop and move forward. Of course, the advice given above assumes that you are arranging an already-existing jazz standard and not your own original composition.

Brainstorming

Now that you've analyzed the tune thoroughly and listened to other versions, you should begin brainstorming by writing verbal descriptions in the two formats detailed below.

Annotate the Lead Sheet

Indicating ideas on the lead sheet is a great way to get started. Just a few words regarding instrumentation, texture, or voicing types can help get the ideas to germinate. As an example, look at the lead sheet in example 10.1 and observe the simple written notes that I've provided. This tune has a medium swing tempo with an AABA form. The written notes deal mostly with the treatment of the melody, but you'll see that I do have an idea about the overall structure of the chart below the lead sheet.

Example 10.1

Create A Schematic Diagram

This is the fun part—where you actually start to create your own arrangement by expanding your thoughts initially developed on the lead sheet. Using your knowledge of song forms, textures, and schematic diagrams (see chapter 3), start the creative process by building a schematic diagram. At this point anything is possible, so let your creative juices flow and enjoy this process. Compromise, which can be frustrating, will come later. Make every effort to get away from your instrument, your computer, and your MP3 player and just hear the arrangement unfold in your mind. Let me reiterate: You should be writing words, not notes, at this stage. In your schematic diagram indicate the form, ideas for orchestration and texture, and the overall scope and contour of the chart. Just brainstorm with pencil in hand, imagining in your mind how the chart will sound and feel.

Example 10.2 contains a schematic diagram of the lead sheet seen above. Notice that the notes from the lead sheet have been transferred to the diagram but with more detail. Also, the entire form is sketched out, again by referring to and expanding upon the preliminary notes from the lead sheet.

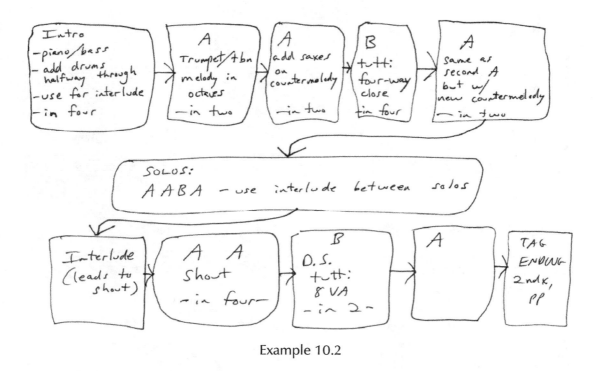

Example 10.2

In the diagram shown above, I have decided to begin with a thin texture of only bass and piano. Also, I intend to reuse the introductory material as an interlude. I'll score the melody for the brass players, with the saxes providing a countermelody during the second A section. At the bridge, I would like for the horns to play in a homophonic manner, and I have even written down the type of chord voicings. The melody concludes with a new countermelody played by the saxes. Furthermore, I have indicated the feel (in four, or in two), and I have also made a note about how I want the chart to integrate the interlude with the solo section. I also intend to include a shout chorus for the first half of the form (the AA section part) with the melody returning for the bridge an octave higher. I am also planning on a tag for the ending. In short, I have made a fairly complete verbal description of the arrangement.

This schematic diagram will not only help me envision the whole arrangement, but it will also serve as a guide as I begin the actual writing. Keep in mind that a schematic diagram is not set in stone. It's just a part of the process that takes place before the arranger starts to make tough decisions concerning instrumentation, tempo, style, blend, etc. Right now as you sketch things out in a general way, there are no limits on what you can do. But later you might hear yourself saying something like this: "Well, that melody note won't work for alto sax like I had planned—I'll give it to the tenor sax instead." Altering your sketch does not mean that your original idea was a bad one; it simply means that you needed to compromise in some way. Regardless of what happens during the actual writing process, having a schematic diagram is still very helpful because it provides the arranger with an overall picture of the entire arrangement.

Transferring Words Into Notation: Three Steps from Sketch to Finished Score

In this section of the chapter, we will explore a three-step process for writing a small group arrangement. We will discuss writing at various levels of detail such as sketching basic ideas, developing your ideas, and creating a full score for a small jazz ensemble.

Of course, you could do all of your music notation on a computer, but there are several creative advantages to using old-fashioned pencil and paper. First of all, it can be difficult to see the arrangement unfold when viewing only a small portion of the arrangement on your computer screen. Also, if you are entering notes on a computer using a piano keyboard, you may be limited by your piano technique. It is important to get away from the keyboard (or any musical instrument) and hear your ideas internally—especially at the beginning stages of the arrangement. Therefore, I strongly urge you to write the old-fashioned way—with pencil and paper. Later, finish the arrangement on the computer.

Let's examine each of three steps that will take us from sketch to finished score.

Step 1: Basic Sketch/Spontaneous Idea Stage

This type of sketching occurs in the earliest stages of writing, although ideas that come along later in the process can be notated quickly in this way as well. Exercise as much spontaneity as you can at this point. You may want to write in an abbreviated manner—the goal is to capture any ideas that come to mind so that they are preserved for possible use later. Basic sketching can be done on a simple piece of staff paper or with whatever kind of paper is nearby when inspiration hits—even a restaurant napkin!

Here is an example of what a handwritten sketch might look like:

Example 10.3

Notice that I did not write a complete score—just raw ideas with labels written next to them. It's a very abbreviated style of getting the ideas on paper. It also includes elements that I first conceived while creating the schematic diagram.

Step 2: Developmental Sketching

Developmental sketching is the next level, where instruments are specified and voicing types are labeled and perhaps scored. Use three-staff sketch paper at this point (available in appendix C), in which the horns are placed in the upper two staves and the rhythm section is consolidated on the bottom staff. You should begin the actual process of voicing the horns and assigning instruments to the various melodies, backgrounds, etc. You may want to write only lead lines (the top voices) with verbal instructions regarding voicing choices (e.g., drop-2, four-way close).

Example 10.4

Step 3: The Finished Score

This next example contains the final score (in concert pitch, with no articulations or dynamics) resulting from the two steps described above. Notice that everything suggested in the developmental sketch (shown above) is included in the score: the brass melody, the sax countermelody, the voicings in measures 5 and 7, and the rhythm section parts.

Example 10.5

Now that we have examined a method for sketching and developing an arrangement, it's time to begin to put pen to paper and begin writing. You'll be arranging several versions of the exercise tunes found in appendix A. These assignments will parallel the study of the example tunes.

Chapter Summary

1. Thoroughly analyze the tune you wish to arrange and listen to other versions of it.
2. Take notes on the lead sheet as you brainstorm.
3. Create a schematic diagram of your arrangement.
4. Refer to the annotated lead sheet and schematic diagram as you:
   (a) Sketch your ideas on staff paper.
   (b) Transfer those ideas to three-staff sketch paper.
   (c) Transfer the three-staff ideas to the finished transposed score.

Assignment 10.1

Annotated Lead Sheets

Create an annotated lead sheet for each of the three exercise tunes located in appendix A. Concentrate on the treatment of the melody—although if you have ideas about an introduction, ending, solo section, etc., include them as well. We'll be learning about those sections in the chapters to come.

Two-Part Writing

In the jazz idiom there is much more collaboration between performer and arranger than in other musical genres. As a result, the jazz performer is crucial to the success of an arrangement. This is especially true for the rhythm section players who are given a certain amount of latitude in interpreting their parts. Horn players, while charged with the duty of blending with one another, understand that jazz interpretation is also an important part of their jobs. Improvised solo sections present perhaps the clearest example of the important role played by the jazz performer. While the arranger provides the chord changes, the rhythmic feel, and possible background parts, the performer is in charge during a solo. So what does a jazz arranger control? It boils down to the following:

- Instrumentation (including ensemble size and choice of instruments)
- Register
- Dynamics
- Articulations
- Tempo

197

- Texture
- Form

With this chapter, we begin deciding how these seven items will be handled. The first step is to choose the wind instruments for the arrangement. You will be learning how to write for two horns and a rhythm section of piano, bass, and drums. Before moving further, let's explore that particular instrumentation in the context of other possibilities.

Instrumentation

This book is called *Arranging for the Small Jazz Ensemble*. What exactly is a small jazz ensemble? The word *ensemble* actually is a French word that means (as a noun) "set" or "group." Or, as an adverb, it means "together." So one would have to assume that the title refers to a musical setting with more than one player. A duo of piano and bass is certainly an ensemble as is two flutes. Another obvious conclusion is that a small jazz ensemble is certainly smaller than a big band. Typically we think of a small jazz ensemble as a rhythm section of piano (and perhaps guitar), bass, drums, or a rhythm section with one or more horn players—but not quite the size of a big band. By horn players I am not referring to French horn players; the term *horn* in a jazz setting is synonymous with wind instruments.

The number of horns used in small groups has varied throughout jazz history. New Orleans "Dixieland" bands normally used three wind instruments—cornet, clarinet, and trombone. The classic bebop ensemble used two horns—often trumpet and alto saxophone (think Dizzy Gillespie and Charlie Parker). Hard bop groups of the 1950s and 1960s such as Art Blakey and the Jazz Messengers normally used three horns. Four or more horns, although seen less frequently, are used with great success on albums such as Horace Silver's album *Hardbop Grandpop*. Miles Davis' *Birth of the Cool* band had nine horns, while Rob McConnell's Tentet used seven horns. Several of these ensemble types are discussed below—all with a rhythm section of piano, bass, and drums.

The Quartet: One Horn and Rhythm Section

The simplest ensemble for beginning jazz arrangers to tackle is one horn plus rhythm section. This instrumentation provides the musicians with the most freedom of expression because the single horn player has no other wind players to blend with. However, even this limited instrumentation calls for decisions to be made. First, what wind instrument will be chosen to join the rhythm section? The type of melodic line (whether rapid, slow moving, wide-ranging, etc.) will affect your choice. This type of writing also requires more decisions about form, rhythm section integration, introductions, endings, how much improvisation, substitute chord changes, etc. In other words, writing for one horn is more complicated than you may have thought.

Assignment 11.1

Writing For One Horn & Rhythm

Arrange one of the exercise tunes located in appendix A for one horn and rhythm section. Write for the horn of your choice (e.g., trumpet, saxophone, or trombone) with piano, bass, and drums as your rhythm section. Your arrangement should consist of only one statement of the melody. Write a transposed score and include rehearsal letters. Refer to the musical suggestions and layout suggestions found at the beginning of chapter 17. Use the score paper provided, your own paper, or notation software.

The Quintet: Two Horns and Rhythm

Writing for two horns demands even more decisions from the arranger—mostly regarding instrumentation (*what* instrument to add) and texture (*how* to add it).

In chapter 4 we learned that instrumental timbre and family are the prime considerations in choosing horns—deciding whether you want the instruments to contrast with one another or to blend in a homogeneous manner. To help you make this critical decision, the following list of two-horn combinations includes audio examples of the ABAC swing exercise tune located in appendix A. Listen carefully to the blend or contrast created by the various combinations. Instrument combinations that blend well are as follows:

1. Trumpet/soprano sax

2. Trumpet/alto sax

3. Trumpet/tenor sax (separated by an octave)

4. Trumpet/trombone (separated by an octave)

5. Trombone/tenor sax

6. Alto sax/tenor sax (separated by an octave)

Contrasting instrumental choices are as follows:

1. Alto sax/trombone (separated by an octave)

2. Trumpet/bari sax (separated by an octave)

Two-horn ensembles still provide opportunities to interpret lines with a great deal of flexibility, especially in a polyphonic texture. In fact, when the two instruments are playing independent lines, it is appropriate for the players to perform their parts in a very individual, almost improvised manner—something that is not possible in large groups.

The Sextet: Three Horns and Rhythm

Three-horn writing is complicated by the fact that one note of a four-note chord struc-ture cannot be played (the pianist can play it, but one note of the chord would need to be left out of the horn voicings). Deciding which chord tone to omit is tricky—this prob-lem is explored further in chapter 13. Three-horn groups certainly can offer the wind players opportunities for individual interpretation of their lines (picture a New Orleans traditional jazz band in which the horns are improvising at the same time). But in more contemporary styles, the increase in horn parts from two to three typically diminishes that freedom. As ensembles increase in size, the importance of the arranger grows as well.

The Septet: Four Horns and Rhythm

Writing for four horns is relatively simple because you can use every note of a four-note chord structure. All the notes of four-way close and drop-2 voicings will be complete with nothing doubled or eliminated. Of course, the accompanying lines should still be scored so that they are tuneful and easy to play. But the reason why this text emphasizes two-horn and four-horn combinations throughout is because these two combinations are the easiest to grasp. In fact, there is a big band arranging technique in which overlapping four-way close voicings are used for the saxophone, trumpet, and trombone sections. Because the saxophone section typically has five saxes, the bari sax part usually doubles the melody an octave below. With this in mind, you can see why understanding four-way close voicing is so important. We will discuss four-horn writing in the next chapter; for now, let's get back to the topic of two-horn arranging.

Two-Horn Writing

As explained in chapter 3, the number of possible textures can be reduced to only two when writing for more than one voice (or horn):

1. Homophonic/Unison
2. Combination

The following melody over a simple ii–V–I progression is scored in unison for two horns (trumpet and alto sax) using the first texture listed above. The melody is on top, with the stems going up. The accompanying voice is scored with the stems going down. In the following example, the melody is scored in unison.

Example 11.9

The example shown above simply changes the color of the instruments by combining them. I had only one decision to make: which instruments to use. In the next example, the melody is harmonized in a homophonic texture.

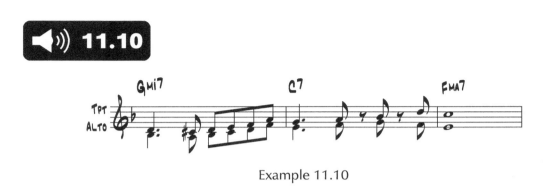

Example 11.10

Notice that in the example shown above the melody is harmonized by the alto sax using the first available chord tone below the melody (a third below) until the last two notes where the harmonization lies a sixth below. Employing thirds throughout would have worked fine, but I decided to use a more stepwise melody for the harmony part as you can see from the last three notes of the alto line: G–F–E.

Writing a Countermelody

Texture two, as described above, indicates that polyphonic writing can be combined with homophony. As a result, sometimes the parts are relatively independent from one another. This means that you will need to develop an important skill: the ability to write an effective countermelody. Composing tuneful countermelodies is among the most challenging skills for beginning arrangers. The countermelody line must complement but not overwhelm the melody, and must also correspond to the harmony of the tune. Keep the following suggestions in mind as you write countermelodies:

1. When the melody is active, write longer accompanying tones or include rests in the countermelody.
2. When the melody is less active, use more rhythmically active lines (write "in the holes").

3. Bring the melody and countermelody together at phrase endings in either unison (or octaves) or in harmony.
4. Search for guide tones (tones that clearly lead the ear through the harmony, such as thirds and sevenths) and incorporate them into your countermelody.
5. Write with simplicity.
6. Contrary motion works well to distinguish the voices.
7. Blues-flavored melodies often work well.

Of the list above, I think that the first three are the most valuable. Writing more active lines in the areas where a melody is less active works very well. As the examples unfold you'll see that my arrangements take advantage of this simple technique in numerous places. Phrase endings are important structural points—bringing the parts together there is very effective.

This next example demonstrates a countermelody accompanying the same simple melody seen in examples 11.9 and 11.10. Notice that when the melodic rhythm slows (the dotted quarter notes), the countermelody moves in eighth notes. Conversely, when the melody moves in eighth notes, the countermelody pauses or rests. The lines converge at the end of the phrase providing a sense of conclusion to the passage. Finally, notice that the countermelody emphasizes guide tones, such as the third and seventh of the Gmi7 chord in the first measure and the sevenths of the C7 and Fma7 in the second and third measures.

Example 11.11

Characteristics of Specific Intervals in Harmony Parts

The study of counterpoint is centered on the relationship between two or more voices. Among the rules of counterpoint are the definitions of consonant and dissonant intervals. While these rules evolved over time, generally speaking, the unison, octave, and fifth are considered perfect consonances. Imperfect consonances include major and minor thirds and sixths. Dissonances include major and minor seconds and sevenths, the perfect fourth, and the tritone.

The following examples illustrate the aural qualities of particular intervals. The perfect consonance of the unison has already been illustrated (see example 11.9). The fifth is another perfect interval. Jazz arrangers, like their classical counterparts, usually avoid writing in parallel fifths, although the part-writing rules are less strict in this regard. The examples below, however, focus on imperfect consonances (thirds and sixths) and on the dissonant intervals (i.e., the perfect fourth, second, and seventh).

These examples are meant to provide insight into how these intervals can be used. However, the intervals chosen for a harmonization normally follow the governing chord progression. You cannot decide arbitrarily to use a certain interval unless you are specifically looking for a particular effect. The harmonization should support and make clear the voice leading of the melody and chords. Also, note that the harmonization is most often placed below the melody.

The following examples illustrate different intervallic harmonizations for a simplified version of the melody used in chapter 3. Listen carefully to the audio tracks as you view the examples.

Thirds and Sixths

Harmonizing in thirds and sixths will provide the most consonant solution. The two intervals often alternate, particularly if a melody rises and falls.

Example 11.12

Parallel Fourths

Harmonizing in parallel fourths conveys a more strident effect that works well in more contemporary jazz styles. Since this melody is rather traditional in nature and the chord progression follows harmonic function, the parallel fourths are blended with thirds in certain places.

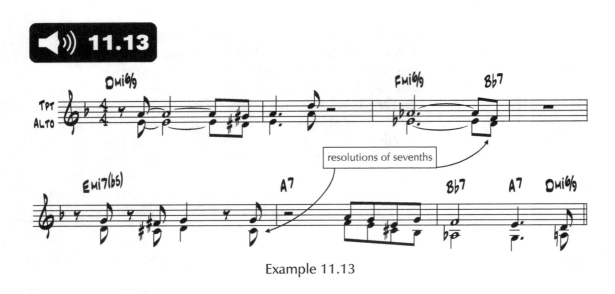

Example 11.13

Notice the resolution of the sevenths in the Fmi7 and Emi7(b5) as they move to their respective dominant chords. In the latter resolution (Emi7b5 to A7 in measure 5), the third and seventh form a tritone on the A7, making the chord movement very clear to the listener.

Sevenths and Seconds

Dissonant intervals, if handled carefully, can assist the listener's ear in following the chord progression. Recall that chord tones that clearly outline the harmony are known as *guide tones*. Usually, guide tones are either thirds or sevenths—but as the next example illustrates, other more dissonant chord tones can be guide tones, too. Notice that this accompanying line is the most independent of the three examples.

Example 11.14

Assignment 11.2

Writing a Countermelody I

Analyze the melody found on the next page which is scored over a ii–V–I–V/ii chord progression in the key of F major. Two countermelody rhythms have been composed in the lower staff with a few notes filled in. Fill in the note heads corresponding to each stem, connecting the given notes. Think about the key and harmonic function—but most of all, compose a line that is tuneful and melodic.

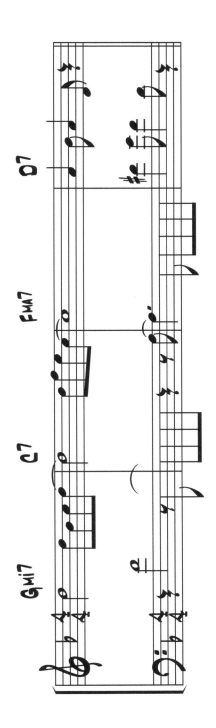

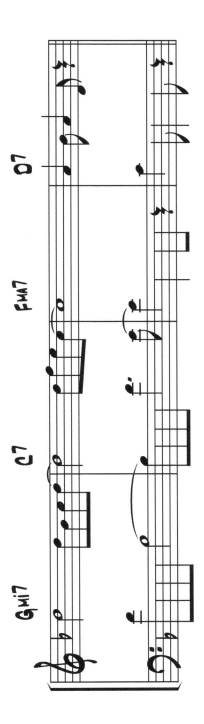

Assignment 11.3

Writing a Countermelody II

On the next page, compose a countermelody that complements the given melody using the suggested rhythms provided on the one-line staff. Provide a harmony part below the melody where the voices match rhythmically. Be sure to listen to the audio recording of the melody.

Hint: The harmony of the example is quite simple—it begins in Eb major, moves to the relative minor through a ii–V–i in C minor, and then modulates to Ab major again through a ii–V–I progression.

Assignment 11.4

Writing a Countermelody III

On the next page, compose a countermelody that complements the given melody using the suggested rhythms provided on the one-line staff. Provide a harmony part below the melody where the voices match rhythmically. Be sure to listen to the audio recording of the melody.

Hint: The chord progression moves from two statements of a ii–V of D to a ii–V of G in measure 5, then to a ii–V–I in C. It concludes with an F7($\sharp$11) chord implying the Lydian $\flat$7 mode.

Example Tunes Harmonized in Two Voices

In keeping with the discussions of previous chapters, "Why Not Now," "Sabrosa," and "December Serenade" will be arranged in the following two textures:

1. Homophonic/unison
2. Combination

Each example is notated in concert pitch and is accompanied with notes of explanation. Articulations and dynamic markings have not been included, but they will be inserted into the final versions in chapter 17. You should probably reacquaint yourself with the lead sheet and analysis of each tune (and the audio recordings) located in chapter 2.

The instruments chosen for these two-horn arrangements vary among the three tunes. I have selected from among the following horns: trumpet, alto sax, and tenor sax. The rhythm section consists of piano, bass and drums. In order to save space, the examples in this chapter do not contain full rhythm section parts; those are notated in the final version of the example tunes in chapter 17.

"Why Not Now" (Homophonic/Unison Texture)

Recall that in chapter 10, "Planning An Arrangement," I suggested a four-step process:

1. Making notes on a lead sheet
2. Creating a schematic diagram of the flow of the entire chart
3. Developmental sketching
4. Final arrangement

As we begin looking at the example tunes, let's examine an annotated lead sheet for a homophonic version of "Why Not Now."

Example 11.17

At this point, I would normally create a schematic diagram of the overall arrangement based on the annotated lead sheet. I would then begin scoring the melody. Since we're only examining the treatment of the melody in this chapter, we won't need to see a diagram of the entire chart. You will see that there are written notes in the score that match the suggestions from the annotated lead sheet.

It was suggested in chapter 2 that "Why Not Now" presents a challenge because of the speed and motion of the melody. For this reason, I have chosen trumpet and alto sax—instruments that can easily negotiate this active melody. Since this is a homophonic texture, the two parts will be in unison or harmony throughout with no independence in the alto line.

Example 11.18

This bebop-style melody works well in a classic trumpet/alto sax duet. The A, B, and D sections are all treated in a very simple manner. The melody is scored in unison for letter A and harmonized in thirds and sixths for sections B and D. The horns revert back to unison beginning with the arpeggio of the Dbmi7 in measure 12, but harmony returns at the cadence (measure 16).

The harmony part of the bridge provides a good example of a guide tone line. In the first four measures (17–20) there are two ii–V–I progressions—one in Gb major and the other in A major. In measure 17, the seventh of the Abmi7 (the Gb) resolves to the third of the Db7 (the F) on the third beat. In measure 19, the seventh of the Bmi7 (the A) resolves to the third of the E7 (the G♯) which in turn remains as the seventh of the Ama7, although the resolution is delayed by the appearance of the F♯ on the "and" of three. Each progression concludes in unison when the tonic chord appears—the Db in measure 18 (anticipated from the previous bar on the "and" of four), and the line in measure 20 (beginning on the "and" of one with the C♯). As in the B and D sections, the harmony is primarily in thirds and sixths.

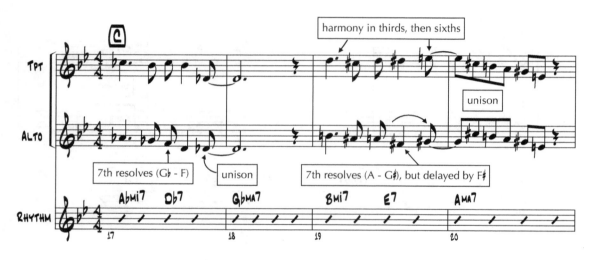

Example 11.19

The bridge concludes with the parts again harmonized in thirds in measures 21–23. In the annotated lead sheet, I've included the suggestion "add scale figure." This Bb major scale leads nicely to the main theme, tying the bridge to the D section.

As you listen to the recording, notice that this arrangement works very well because of its simplicity. Harmonizing in consonant intervals like thirds and sixths is perhaps the most common approach to take when writing for two horns. The next example is more complex because there is a countermelody scored for the trumpet.

"Why Not Now" (Combination Texture)

The combination texture of "Why Not Now" for two horns offers the horn players more flexibility in their interpretation as the audio track makes clear. The alto sax is the primary melody instrument—the trumpet does not enter until letter B so that the arrangement builds momentum as it progresses. Notice that there are substitute chords in the B and D sections that correspond to the accompanying trumpet line. These changes will be discussed below.

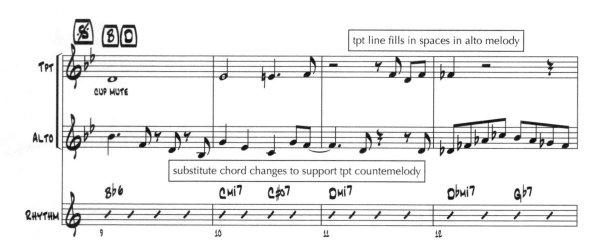

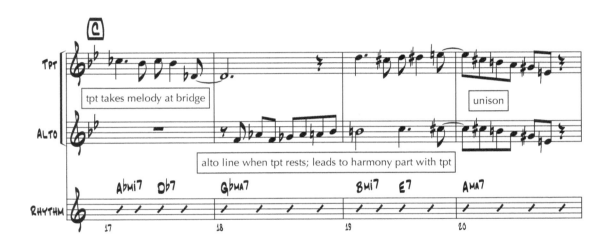

Example 11.20

The alto sax plays the melody in this version which includes a countermelody played by a muted trumpet. The trumpet line guides the listener's ear through the substituted harmony mentioned earlier. Arrangers and performers often use a I–ii–♯ii°–iii progression for the first two measures of the A section in tunes based on "I Got Rhythm" changes.

Notice that the subsequent trumpet lines in the B section merely fill in the gaps in the alto melody, thus keeping clear of the melodic statement. The lines do converge in unison in measure 16, ending the first half of the melody.

In the bridge (letter C), the instruments switch roles. This is a very common device used by arrangers at major structural points in a piece. As the trumpet takes the melody, the alto assumes the accompaniment role. The bridge contains a variety of textures: the horns complement each other contrapuntally in the first phrase (measures 17–18), end the second phrase in unison (measure 20), and finally are voiced homophonically for the last phrase (measures 21–23) where the alto is a third below. The final section (D) is identical to letter B, as was the case in the homophonic version.

"Sabrosa" (Homophonic/Unison Texture)

Like "Why Not Now," "Sabrosa" is in AABA song form—but each section is sixteen bars instead of eight. The homophonic arrangement in the example shown below features the alto saxophone, although the trumpet does take the lead when the instruments are in harmony. Notice the blend of rhythmic notation and slash notation in the condensed rhythm section part.

Example 11.21

"Sabrosa" is arranged with the same instrumentation as "Why Not Now" beginning with the alto sax alone on the melody, like the combination texture version of "Why Not Now." The trumpet joins the alto sax in unison on the second statement of the melody, but as they break into harmony beginning in measure 25, the alto sax is used as the harmonizing instrument.

In this next example, we see that the alto line is constructed of a stepwise descent from the F in measure 25 to the B♭ four bars later with one leap up to F in measure 27. Are these guide tones? Do they reveal the harmony in combination with the melody? Try playing this example on the piano and I think you'll hear the harmony unfold, and even more so if you play the bass notes along with the two-horn lines. This is an excellent example of smooth voice leading.

Example 11.22

The bridge (letter C) again features the alto sax on the melody, so in this arrangement the instruments don't switch roles as they did for the bridge of "Why Not Now." The trumpet joins the alto sax in unison in measure 41, breaking into harmony (with the trumpet on top) two bars later. Letter D, which is the last statement of the primary melody, is harmonized in thirds. Notice that the eighth note line in measures 48 and 52 is in unison, giving much more clarity to the rapid line.

"Sabrosa" (Combination Texture)

The combination texture of "Sabrosa" in the next example is scored with the same instruments. It shares a few things in common with the homophonic version such as the descending line illustrated in the previous example.

Example 11.23

This version features the trumpet on the melody with a rhythmically contrasting alto sax countermelody entering at letter B.

The countermelody, illustrated in example 11.24 below, begins on beat 2 of measure 17 where there is a rhythmic gap in the trumpet melody. The line concludes with an A minor scale passage followed by an ascending augmented fifth interval in measure 20. The color tones of the chord changes are emphasized, primarily the eleventh of the Gmin chord (the C) and the E from the C/Ab chord. Once again the countermelody fills in the gap of the melody in measure 21 where the seventh of the Gmi7 (the F) resolves to the E, the third of the C7.

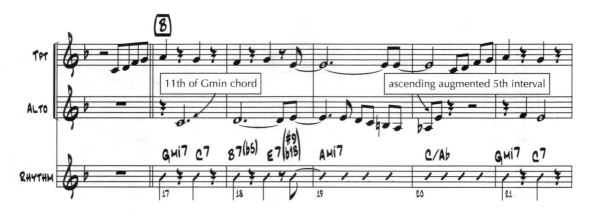

Example 11.24

The horns come together in harmony in the sixth bar of B leading to the bridge. Letter C is scored with the trumpet on the melody with the alto entering on a sweeping ascending line in measure 39. This is another good illustration of writing "in the holes" of the melody. Also notice the simplicity of this line—merely a Db major scale rising in quarter notes. As the parts converge, the horns are harmonized as they were in the homophonic version until letter D where the horns are voiced in unison rather than harmonically.

Example 11.25

"December Serenade" (Homophonic/Unison Texture)

The final tune discussed in this chapter is the ballad "December Serenade." The piece is in modified ABAC form in which the final section is only four bars long. In arranging a ballad for a small ensemble, it is appropriate to score the melody as a featured solo for one horn in order to individualize the interpretation of the melodic line, particularly during the initial melodic statement. This melody would lend itself to many instrumental possibilities; I have chosen trumpet for this version. Note also the choice of the darker timbre of the tenor sax instead of the alto. Example 11.26 contains the homophonic/unison version.

Example 11.26

The homophonic version above excludes the accompanying horn until the repeat of the melody at letter C. At that point, the tenor sax harmonizes the melody in thirds and sixths. Since the melody is sequential, the harmonization is identical in measures 17–18 and 19–20; it just moves down a step. Notice that the colorful ♯11 is included in the tenor part for the B♭ and A♭ dominant sevenths. The blues line that concludes the melody is scored in octaves. A chromatic descending guide tone line would also have been effective. The choice of tenor sax for the accompanying voice was one I really pondered. I knew there would be sections of this arrangement that would be in the upper register of the horn, but that's what I wanted—the strident sound of the tenor sax high register. You can really hear it on the concert B♭ in measure 22. It adds a poignant quality to the passage.

"December Serenade" (Combination Texture)

Arranging "December Serenade" in a combination texture was relatively simple—the whole notes in the melody were the perfect places to write countermelodies.

Example 11.27

Both the combination version and homophonic version begin with the trumpet stating the melody alone with the tenor sax entering at letter C. In the combination texture above, the tenor sax answers the trumpet with an ascending countermelody in quarter note triplets. Notice that the triplets give the line an improvisatory, free flavor.

The next example illustrates the relationship between the parts. The tenor line begins an octave below the trumpet's whole note (G) and it begins rhythmically on the second quarter note of a quarter note triplet adding to the answering effect. The relationship is repeated as the melody moves down sequentially in measures 19 and 20.

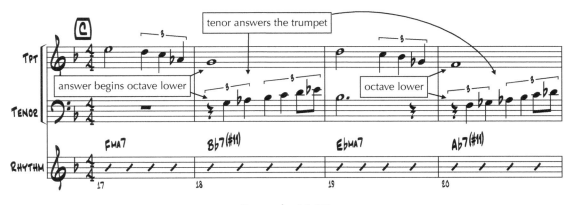

Example 11.28

The parts converge at the Cmi11 as the melody nears its end, using the same harmonization as the homophonic version.

Conclusion

Writing for two horns and rhythm section is a great way to start learning the craft of jazz arranging. The issues dealt with in this section of the book (primarily textures, composing tuneful countermelodies, and instrumental blend) are relevant regardless of the size of the group you are writing for. The next chapter is devoted to four-horn writing. There, you'll see that the arrangements in this chapter are simply expanded to accommodate the larger ensemble resulting in new instrumental colors.

Chapter Summary

1. Write either homophonically (which includes unison and octaves) or with countermelodies combined with homophonic sections.
2. The harmonization should support the voice leading of the melody and chords.
3. When writing a countermelody, compose lines that compliment the melody but do not conflict with it. When the melody is active, write longer accompanying tones or include rests in the countermelody. When the melody is less active, use more rhythmically active lines.
4. When writing contrapuntally, the parts often converge at phrase endings.
5. Reverse the roles of the instruments for the bridge section.

Assignment 11.5

Two-Horn Arranging

Select one of the exercise tunes located in appendix A. Create two two-horn arrangements of this tune: one using the homophonic/unison texture and the other using the combination texture. Use staff paper with three staves. Put the horns on the top two staves and the rhythm section on the bottom staff. Refer to the annotated lead sheet you completed in assignment 10.1. Helpful hints for each tune are included in appendix A.

12

Four-Part Writing

With this chapter, our band has grown by two players. You'll notice two things about the examples in this chapter: First, the instrumentation is always trumpet, alto sax, tenor sax, trombone, piano, bass, and drums. Second, the arrangements are basically the same as they were in the last chapter, but thickened with two additional horns.

We learned in the last chapter that writing for four horns is relatively simple because four-part chords are always complete (no chord tones need to be eliminated) and no chord tones have to be doubled. So writing with four-way close and the related drop-2 voicings involves merely notating the voicings in the proper ranges for each instrument. However, it is also important to realize that the more advanced voicing techniques (e.g., quartal, "So What," and slash chords) are available as well with a larger group of horns.

As we work with our expanded group there will be a variety of voicing and approach options. Therefore, this might be a good time for you to review the chapters in the book that deal with those subjects. Pay close attention to chapter 9 in particular as you review the various approach techniques. Having the voicings and approach methods fresh in your mind will benefit you greatly as we make our way through this chapter.

Some of the same material introduced in the last chapter will be revisited here. Example 12.1 contains the same simple melody over an F major ii–V–I progression that was used previously to illustrate textures. Here it is thickened with additional voices in a four-horn instrumentation. It is written in SATB format so you can easily see the motion of each voice. In the previous chapter, the melody of this tune was scored in unison. Here, however, it is scored in octaves with the trumpet and alto sax in unison and the trombone and tenor sax in unison an octave below.

Example 12.1

In the next example, this same melody is scored homophonically (i.e., every tone of the melody is harmonized). For this reason, we must be careful as we choose and apply the right approach techniques, even in an example as simple as this one. As you view and listen to the example, notice the smooth voice leading. Pay close attention to the shift from four-way close voicings to open position chords occurring in the second measure under the melody notes Bb and D.

Example 12.2

While the discussion at the moment is focused on texture, we can analyze the voicing and approach types, too. In the first measure the melody is scored with four-way close voicings. For the C♯, since the melody is chromatic at this point, the approach type is chromatic parallel. For the scale passage, the approach type is diatonic. Notice that after the C♯ melody note, there are no accidentals in any voice—this indicates that this passage is diatonic and all in the key of F major.

The second measure continues the same voicings and diatonic approach technique, but as the melody leaps to the D on the "and" of four the voicing type changes to drop-2. At this same location in chapter 11, the two horns switched from harmonizing in thirds to sixths to improve the voice leading of the accompanying line (see example 11.2). In example 12.2, the whole note is scored with a quartal voicing. Notice that the chord symbol indicates Fma7. The voicing, however, forms an F6/9. Remember that the sixth is a possible substitution choice for the seventh—and if you use the sixth and ninth it forms a quartal chord. If you need to review this, refer to the chord tone substitution chart in chapter 6.

The next example resembles example 11.3 in which there is a combination of a countermelody (or polyphony) and homophony at the end of the phrase. The difference here is that the melody and countermelody are thickened with an additional horn on each line, and the end of the phrase is scored with four-part chords, identical to example 12.2.

Example 12.3

As these examples demonstrate, writing for four or more voices is often simply an expansion of the two-voice process. Often the primary ideas develop with two voices in mind. The addition of more voices is achieved by applying the appropriate voicings (e.g., tertian, drop-2, quartal, etc.) and approach methods. Naturally, with more voices may come new and different compositional ideas. The example tunes illustrated in this chapter, however, primarily involve an expansion of the two-voice versions seen in chapter 11.

Example Pieces Harmonized in Four Voices

The melodies of the example tunes are presented below in condensed scores in the same two textures as in chapter 11: homophonic/unison and combination. The instrumentation for all the versions consists of a horn section of trumpet, alto sax, tenor sax, and trombone. For most of the examples, the trumpet and alto sax share the top horn staff, and the tenor sax and trombone share the bottom staff. SATB stem directions are used, so that each horn part can be followed easily. The rhythm section parts are again condensed into one staff.

"Why Not Now" (Homophonic/Unison Texture)

You'll immediately hear and see some similarities with the two-horn homophonic track since the featured instruments are trumpet and alto sax. Unison and harmony in thirds and sixths predominate. As you listen, notice the change in texture as the lower horns enter on the bridge (letter C).

Example 12.4

Like its two-horn counterpart, the melody in this example is scored in unison during the first melodic statement and is harmonized a third below beginning at letter B. However, the rapid eighth note line in measures 12–15 is scored in unison and the concluding line (measure 16) is harmonized, again exactly like the two-horn version. The lower horns enter at letter C, as the ensemble is scored in four-part harmony, mostly with drop-2 voicings. Example 12.5 illustrates the passage as it moves from drop-2 to four-way close on the "and" of four in measure 17. The most common reason for switching between open and close positions is the presence of a leap in the melody. Also notice the ♭9 over the D♭7 chord, the chromatic approaches in measure 19, and the diatonic approaches in measure 20.

If you have some basic keyboard ability, you should play this passage slowly, observing how each voice moves. This short passage reveals how much thought must go into every musical decision.

Important!

The most common reason for switching between open and close voicings is the presence of a leap in the melody.

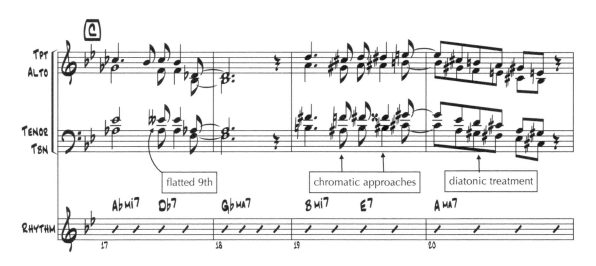

Example 12.5

The bridge ends with the rapid line in measures 21–22 written in unison as it sits in a good range for all instruments. Four-part harmony is used for the half cadence in measure 23. The D.S. sends the form back to B (labeled D) like the two-horn version.

Remember that as you progress through this chapter you'll begin to see that much of the creative process can be thought of in just two parts. The arrangements in this chapter simply expand upon the decisions made when thinking of a two-part texture.

"Why Not Now" (Combination Texture)

In order to help you see the independent lines in this version of "Why Not Now," I have provided a more complete score (the rhythm section parts are still condensed). There is also a horn reduction provided for the last phrase of the bridge in order to examine a variety of approach techniques. You'll see that for this arrangement, I've separated the brass and saxes into two distinct "sections" of the band. The sax "section" performs the melody at letters A, B, and D; the brass "section" takes the bridge melody.

tpt and tbn harmonize bridge melody;
alto and tenor play counter line in octaves

unison

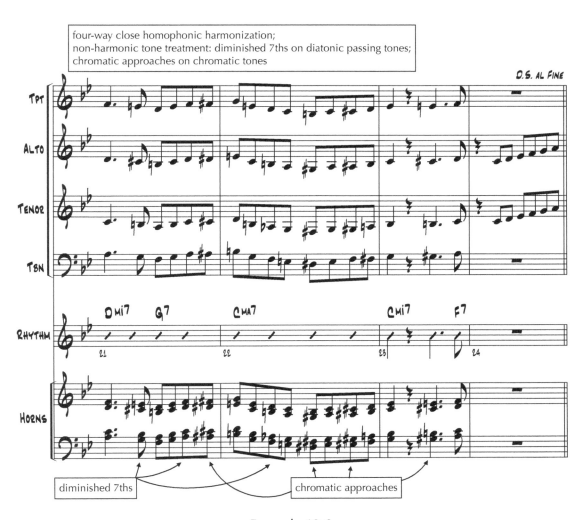

Example 12.6

Notice that the countermelodies are identical to those written for the two-horn combination arrangement. However, there are some interesting areas in the bridge (letter C) to examine where the versions diverge. First, notice in example 12.6 that when the brass instruments take over the melody from the saxes in measure 17, they are in two-part harmony. This was written for a single instrument in the two-horn version. The final phrase of the bridge (measures 21–23) is scored in parallel thirds in the two-horn version. In the four-horn version above, it is scored in four-part harmony. Refer to the horn reduction staff on the third page of example 12.6. The passing tones are harmonized with diminished and chromatic approaches. This same passage was used in chapter 9, "Nonharmonic Tones," to demonstrate various approach methods. Compare the version in the example shown above with those in chapter 9 (examples 9.10, 9.11, and 9.12). You'll see that they are all slightly different, but I think that the solution demonstrated above works best.

"Sabrosa" (Homophonic/Unison Texture)

As we examine the four-horn version of "Sabrosa" we will see the same process as before—the two-horn versions have merely been thickened with the additional two voices. In this version, you'll see that changes in instrumentation provide momentum as unison horns shift into two-part harmony and culminate in four-part scoring. Listen for those texture changes as you examine the arrangement.

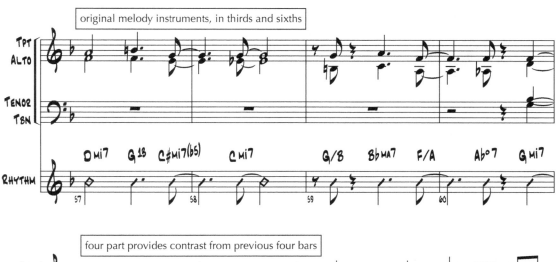

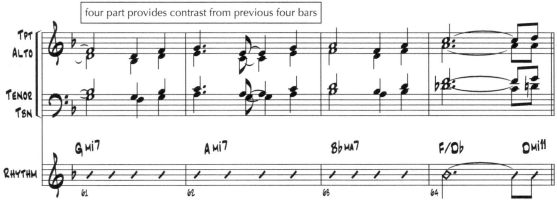

Example 12.7

The version in the previous example features the two upper instruments on the initial melody in unison. At letter B, the other horns enter a third below, similar to letter D of the two-voice version. In example 12.8 below there is a comparison between the two-horn and four-horn versions of measures 25–28. You will notice that both are in two parts, but the harmony part begins a sixth below the melody rather than a third in the four-horn version. Both versions utilize primarily guide tones (thirds and sevenths), but the example illustrates that there is more than one solution available.

Example 12.8

As the piece approaches the bridge, the variety of instrumental textures helps to propel the arrangement. In measure 28, the horns divide into four-way close voicings leading to the bridge (letter C), scored only for alto sax. The final eight bars of the bridge are harmonized first in two parts, then thickened to four. Letter D, the return of the primary theme, is orchestrated with even more rapid changes in texture. The melody is first harmonized in four-way close (measures 49–56), then in two parts using the original melody instruments (measures 57–60), and finally in four-way close voicings to conclude the melody.

"Sabrosa" (Combination Texture)

The four-horn combination texture version is similar to the two-horn version and also has sections in common with the four-horn homophonic version just described.

The instruments are utilized much as they are in the homophonic version, with trumpet and alto sax taking the melody at letters A and B. When the lower instruments enter at B, however, they perform the same countermelody as seen in the two-horn combination version.

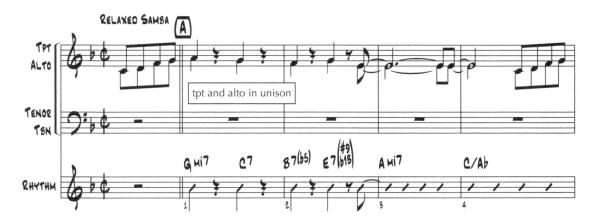

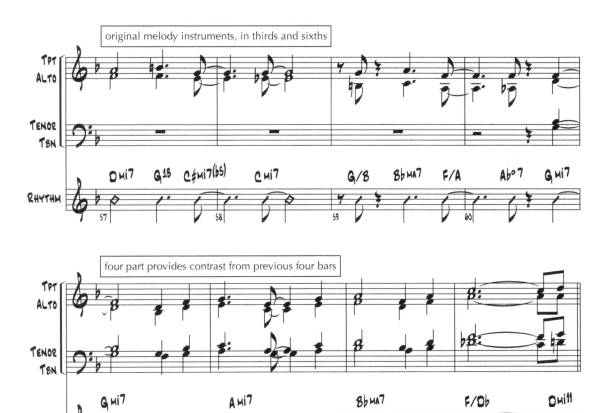

Example 12.9

The version presented above provides another excellent example of using instrumentation to build intensity. The countermelody introduced at letter B (measure 17) merges with the melody in measure 22, remaining in two parts in order to strengthen the melody.

As in the homophonic version, a four-part section follows in measure 28 leading to the bridge which is written for the alto sax. The identical countermelody that was used in the two-voice combination version (example 11.23) is also scored here, this time for tenor sax and trombone. The simplicity of the line (a D♭ major scale in quarter notes) provides an appealing rhythmic contrast to the syncopated melody. The example ends in the same manner as the homophonic version with the textural contrast of letter D.

"December Serenade" (Homophonic/Unison Texture)

When performing jazz ballads, solo horn players typically interpret their melodic lines in an individual fashion. Therefore, you may find that the ballad example, "December Serenade," works best in either of the two-part textures demonstrated in the previous chapter. As an ensemble increases in size, the role of the horn players expands. They must still play with the appropriate style, but must compromise their individual concepts of how the line should be played for the sake of blending with the players around them—playing lines in a personal manner is no longer possible. However, on the positive side, voicing the rich harmony of this piece in four parts provides more harmonic possibilities expressed by the horns—voicings that were not available with only two horns. Listen for the expanded harmonic role played by the horns in the following four-horn versions.

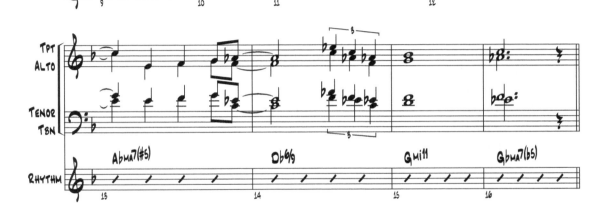

Example 12.10

I originally conceived of this version of "December Serenade" as a trumpet feature. The trumpet solo expands into four-part writing in the ninth measure. In the example below, examine the chromatic harmonization of the descending line in measure 11. The approach method used here is slightly different from the normal procedure when harmonizing a chromatic line in which a target tone is identified and approached chromatically in all parts. In this case, the chromatic lines in each part are derived from the initial chord rather than the target chord (the Eb7sus4) so that the richness of consecutive suspended chord harmony results.

Example 12.11

The alto sax thickens the texture as it joins the trumpet in the restatement of the melody at letter C. The example concludes with four-part harmony leading to octaves on the blues line which ends the melody.

"December Serenade" (Combination Texture)

The combination texture version of "December Serenade" is very similar to the homophonic version. The countermelody used in the two-part version is added to letter C and is scored for the two lower instruments.

Example 12.12

This more interesting contrapuntal version begins identically to the homophonic version. However, it includes the beautiful countermelody seen earlier in the two-horn combination version (example 11.27) beginning at letter C scored for the lower instruments. The trumpet and alto sax play the melody in octaves at this point rather than in two-part harmony as in the homophonic example. After the countermelody is introduced, this version concludes in the same manner as the previous four-horn homophonic version.

Conclusion

Writing for four horns and rhythm section is a great way to explore the possibilities of voicings and approach techniques. Even though these examples simply expand the two-horn versions in most cases, they contain correct voicing and approaches that take careful thought and planning. Even one misplaced note can ruin an arrangement. Often, this is the result of an incorrect voicing, an awkward approach technique, or misuse of open or close voicing options. Next we'll examine the challenge of three-horn writing. Although we once again will use the basic structure of the two-horn versions, the chapter will focus on adapting the four-horn arrangements into three horns.

Chapter Summary

1. Four-part writing is often just the expansion of a two-part concept.
2. You should clearly understand voicing and approach procedures in order to write for four horns.
3. Writing with more voices means less freedom for the players, but it does offer more possibilities for the arranger in terms of texture and timbre.

Assignment 12.1

Four-Horn Arranging

Expand one of your two-horn arrangements into a four-horn version. Use trumpet, alto sax, tenor sax, trombone, and a rhythm section of piano, bass, and drums.

13

Three-Part Writing

While I was writing this book, I thought it was important to include detailed chapters on two-part writing (in which the arranger thinks in terms of interweaving dual lines) and four-part writing (in which complete chords can be scored). However, three-horn jazz ensembles are very common, and arrangers must be ready to deal with the unique challenge of three-part writing. Writing for three voices is more difficult than writing for either two or four voices. In a style in which four-part chords are the norm (root, third, fifth, and seventh, along with their possible substitutions) one chord tone must be omitted when writing for three horns. There are several considerations to keep in mind when writing for three voices: which chord tone will be eliminated, the type of chord structure, and most importantly, the flow of each individual line.

Three-Part Voicing Structures

There are three structures that I use when writing for three horns: shell voicings, simple triads, and quartal voicings. Like any voicing, these can be inverted. An inverted quartal voicing in particular produces interesting whole step clusters that will be discussed below. So while writing in three parts can feel a little constricting (as you decide which tone to omit), these voicings offer simple solutions to the arranging challenges you'll face. Remember that the flow of each line is the most critical element, especially since the effect will be more transparent than in a four-voice texture.

Shell Voicings

Shell voicings were introduced in chapter 6 through a series of keyboard exercises. There we learned that the third and seventh are fundamental tones, and that one extra "color tone"—often the fifth or ninth—is included. Obviously, when compared with a four-way close voicing, there is a note missing—so these work well when writing in three parts. The root is the most expendable chord tone since the bass supplies it.

Example 13.1

Triads

While a simple triad is somewhat unusual in a jazz setting, it is sometimes the best choice if you are looking for a clean and simple sonority. Obviously, a C triad will perfectly express a C chord but will add no additional color or tension. Three-note chords can also be opened up by using drop-2, as we observed in our discussion of four-voice structures.

Close Voicing   Drop-2 Voicing

Example 13.2

Triad structures are often utilized as the top three notes of a slash chord, supplying the tones of the upper symbol. For example, a Bb13(b9) chord can be voiced as a G/Bb7 slash chord. The three horns would play the G triad while the rhythm section plays the entire chord. There are more of these structures illustrated in chapter 8, "Slash Chords."

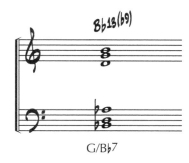

Example 13.3

Quartal Voicings and Clusters

Often, two fourths are stacked one on top of the other, thereby forming a quartal structure. These chords can be inverted just like any other chord. Doing so creates interesting whole steps, either on top of the chord (x) or on the bottom (y). The inverted structures (x and y) can be thought of as "cluster" voicings because of the close proximity of two of the voices.

Example 13.4

Three-voice dominant seventh chords are often scored with a perfect fourth over a tritone. This is a very common left hand piano shell voicing (and another good voicing to practice on a keyboard).

Example 13.5

Example Tunes Voiced in Three Parts

I have chosen a couple of interesting locations in "Why Not Now" and "December Serenade" to illustrate how to arrange using three voices. I've chosen places in those tunes
that were scored in four voices in the previous chapter, so you'll be referred back to
chapter 12 from time to time.

"Why Not Now"

In reviewing the four-voice versions of "Why Not Now," you'll recall that there are parts
that are simply thickened versions of the two-horn examples—places where the two
lines are doubled. These sections are easy to convert to a three-horn arrangement because one horn can be removed from the accompanying line. Let's assume that our
instrumentation is trumpet, alto sax, tenor sax, and rhythm section. With this instrumentation, letter B of the combination texture would like this:

Example 13.6

If you compare this example with example 12.6 (from the chapter on four-voice writing), you'll see that the trombone part which was doubling the trumpet line is eliminated. The melody, being the most important line, is still voiced with two instruments.

The next example provides a three-note variation of letter C from example 12.6, which is the bridge of "Why Not Now." Again, a review of 12.6 shows that this section begins in three parts—the brass are in harmony and the saxes are in unison. By shifting parts around, the music remains basically unchanged. The trombone part from the four-part version has been moved to the alto. There are drop-2 tertian voicings in the third and fourth measures of the example. The third measure in particular illustrates an effective flow in each of the lower two parts.

Example 13.7

"December Serenade"

The three-horn example of "December Serenade" illustrates a combination of tertian and quartal approaches. The horns in the first and third measures of example 13.8 below are scored with second inversion triads. Note that the first voicing (the Fma7) is voiced with a C major triad in the horns—E,C, G, from the top down. The voices move diatonically parallel toward a dominant quartal voicing in measures 2 and 4 of the example (and approached chromatically on the last quarter note of the preceding quarter note triplet). The second phrase (measures 5–8) begins with cluster voicings, moves to quartal, then to octaves, and finally to a tertian structure. These voicings are indicated in the example.

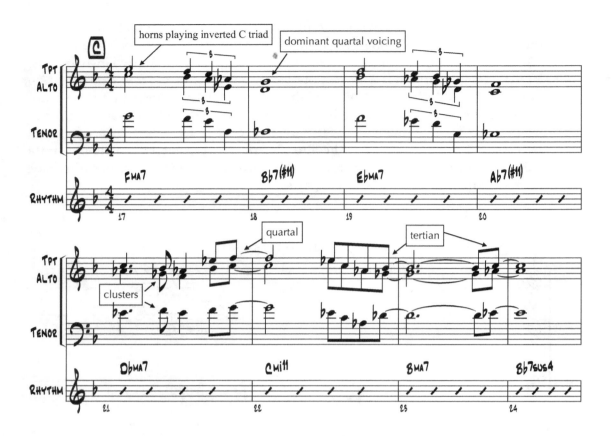

Example 13.8

There will be additional three-voice examples in chapter 17 in which the background parts of "Sabrosa" are scored for three horns while supporting an alto solo.

Conclusion

We have now explored the treatment of the melody in two-horn, three-horn, and four-horn combinations. The next step is to explore the other sections that constitute a complete arrangement. This means that we will be adding the sections that require some actual composition on your part (i.e., introductions, endings, interludes, solo sections, solo backgrounds, and shout/soli sections). Fortunately there are standard ways of dealing with these important components. In the next chapter we will use the example pieces to study the art of the introduction.

Chapter Summary

1. Three-part writing is more difficult than either two-horn or four-horn writing.
2. There are three considerations when writing for three parts: which chord tone to omit from a four-part voicing, the structure (shell voicing, triad, or quartal voicing), and the flow of each line.

Assignment 13.1

Three-Horn Arranging

Alter the four-horn versions of the exercise tunes by eliminating either the alto sax, tenor sax, or trombone part. Continue to write a condensed rhythm section part.

Introductions

It takes creativity to arrange an existing melody because you must determine voicing types, approach methods, and countermelodies. But the introduction and ending involve an even higher level of creativity because these two often related sections are usually comprised of material that is newly composed. For this reason, these next two chapters of the book were perhaps the most enjoyable for me to write because they really tapped into my creative side. As you go through the material, you'll see that I have taken three of the example tunes and composed a variety of introductions and endings. It was fun to see how many ways I could begin and end the same three tunes. I also remember the smiles on the musicians' faces as they recorded these particular examples—perhaps predicting what intro or ending technique would be coming next.

The introduction is vital to an arrangement; obviously it is the first musical event that occurs. The introduction needs to match the style, tempo, rhythmic feel, and overall essence of the tune to which it is attached. Not only does the introduction begin the piece, it is also likely that the material you choose for the intro will come back somewhere else in the arrangement. Often, the arranger can construct endings, introductions, and interludes from the same material. Not all pieces require a formal introduction—sometimes an improvised section leading to the melody will do the job. The introduction is frequently the last section composed because it can be constructed with material from the arrangement. You'll see examples of this technique in some of the upcoming examples.

Common Introduction Types

Introductions can be categorized and labeled. Each technique will be explained throughout this chapter. Common introduction types are:

- Improvised introductions
- Last section of the melody (often the last four bars)
- Vamp (a repeating series of a few chords)
- Melodic fragment used to construct introduction
- Unrelated material (a completely new section)

Style Considerations

The five introduction types listed above can be further categorized by the style of the tune. The following chart combines introductions and styles/tempos in order to help narrow the choice of introduction. Obviously this list does not contain every possibility, but it does provide some initial ideas about how to begin an arrangement.

Common Introductions

Style	Types of Introduction Common to That Style
Up-Tempo Swing	Improvised introduction Melodic fragment Unrelated material
Medium Swing	Last section of melody Melodic fragment Unrelated material
Ballad	Last section of melody Vamp Improvised introduction (piano or guitar, *rubato*)
Latin	Vamp (by far the most common) Last section of melody Melodic fragment Unrelated material

Improvised Introductions

Beginning with an improvised solo is an effective way to make the listener comfortable with the feel and groove of the piece. The soloist will usually play the entire form of the tune, sometimes even playing several choruses. It is very common in tunes with authentic or modified "I Got Rhythm" changes such as "Why Not Now," and it is also common at fast tempos.

Improvised Solo by a Horn, Piano, or Guitar

Using a rhythm section instrument such as piano or guitar often works best to provide a contrast with the melody if that melody is scored for the horns, although a horn could also fulfill this role. In this particular example, the pianist introduces the song by playing one entire chorus as a solo.

   (No notation shown)

Drum Solo

Drum solo introductions can either be in time or out of time. Those played in time are often performed only on the hi-hat, especially on fast swing tunes. It also sets up the tempo and feel for the listener while revealing nothing else about the piece. As a result, it provides the most anticipation for the listeners as they wait for the melody to appear. Is it in major or minor? Is the melody lyrical or angular? An introduction by the drummer cannot provide any of this information. As you listen to this next example, imagine that you're hearing "Why Not Now" for the first time.

   (No notation shown)

Rubato Piano/Guitar Solo

The next example could actually fit into two categories. It is an improvised solo introduction but it is derived from the last section of the tune. In this example, you'll hear the last portion of the first half of the ballad "December Serenade" played as a rubato piano solo. Refer to the lead sheet to get your bearings; this is section B where the suspended chords ascend. Often the pianist or guitarist plays the entire tune in a rubato manner, but just as often he or she will only play a specific section of the tune. This part of the tune works well for a rubato introduction because of the richness of the suspended chord harmony. The pianist is instructed to set up the time as the introduction concludes—listen to the way he interprets those instructions.

Example 14.3

Last Section of Melody

This approach, in which the last four or eight bars of the piece are played as an introduction, is extremely common. This method sets the mood of the piece without giving away the opening melody. On a "club date" job (a setting in which the performers are essentially background to a larger event) it is almost always played by the pianist alone. In an arrangement, this approach provides more opportunities to involve the other instruments.

The previous example illustrates two introduction techniques: it is an improvised solo, but also is constructed of material from the melody. There, the pianist introduced the tune by playing the entire B section of the tune as a rubato solo—but "December Serenade" has yet another useful segment that can be used as introductory material: this time, it's the actual last line of the tune where the blues scale occurs. The next example demonstrates this technique but this time with the pianist playing in tempo.

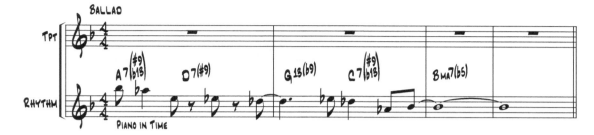

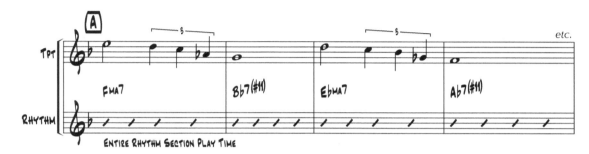

Example 14.4

The next two examples illustrate how effective a simplified version of the last four measures can work. First, here are the last four measures of "Why Not Now" concluding with a half cadence (the F7 chord).

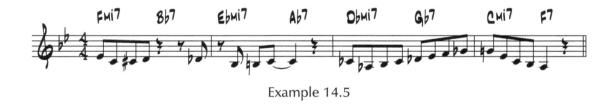

Example 14.5

In using this material for the introduction, I decided to eliminate the fast-moving eighth note lines (I didn't want to give that away to the listener so early in the arrangement) and instead used the harmony voiced for the entire horn section.

The example shown below illustrates this technique. Notice the guide tone line in the melody (sevenths resolving to thirds). As you listen to the audio track, observe how dynamic and exciting it is to begin with the entire band playing stop-time (that's when the entire group plays identical rhythms and the drummer and bassist cease their normal time-keeping roles). If this were an actual arrangement (instead of just an example), I would want to use this introductory material again later—perhaps as an interlude or an ending.

Example 14.6

Another good technique to use when extracting an introduction from the last section of the melody is *instrument layering*. In the next example, the introduction of "Sabrosa" begins with piano, and the other instruments of the rhythm section enter in layers. Since it has a sixty-four bar form, the introduction shown below is constructed of the last eight bars of the form rather than the last four. Listen as the drums and bass enter on beat 4 of the measure—this adds rhythmic interest to the introduction.

Example 14.7

Vamp

A vamp is a repeating series of a few chords often utilizing the harmony that begins the piece. It is commonly found in Latin styles such as bossa novas and sambas. It sets the stage for the feel of the tune and hints at the tonality without revealing the melody. The most common examples of this technique, again heard often in "club date" settings, are either a repeating sequence of I–bII7 chords with each chord lasting one measure, or a ii–V repeating pattern, again with each chord lasting one measure.

I–bII7 Vamp

The bII7 chord, as you should recall from your jazz theory study, functions as a tritone substitution for the V7 chord. As a result, a I–bII7 vamp is essentially a I–V7 repeating pattern but with smoother motion in the bass. In this next example, the I–bII7 progression scored for piano and bass serves an introduction for the tune "Sabrosa." It is effective to have the drums enter with the horns as the melody arrives, solidifying the time and feel.

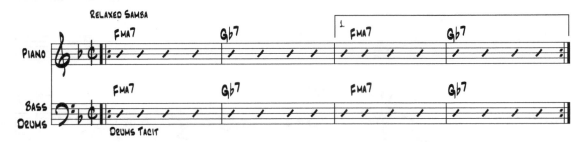

Example 14.8

ii–V Vamp

The term *ii–V vamp* refers to the ii and V chords of the home key. This common vamp can actually be thought of in two ways, either diatonically or modally. For example, a repeating Dmi7–G7 pattern establishes the key of C because both chords are part of the C major diatonic tonality. However, some jazz theorists prefer to think of D as the home tonality—in other words, if you were going to play Dmi7–G7 on the piano, you'll probably hear D as the tonic because the progression never resolves to C. In that case, a i–IV progression results, establishing the D Dorian mode as the home tonality. Both analyses are valid. I'll be using the ii–V vamp label as I describe the next example.

In example 14.9, a ii–V vamp serves as the introduction to "Sabrosa." Layering is used here, similar to example 14.8 in which the rest of the rhythm section joins the pianist halfway through the introduction.

Example 14.9

This exciting introduction is yet another example of introductory material that could be reused somewhere else in the arrangement.

You may find other sections of the piece that provide harmonic material for a vamp. The chord sequence that concludes the first half of "December Serenade" is a colorful alternative to the more conventional I–bII and ii–V sequences described above.

In this next example, the introduction is made up of a vamp using the last two chords of the first half of the tune. It also layers the entrance of the rhythm section instruments seen in several earlier examples.

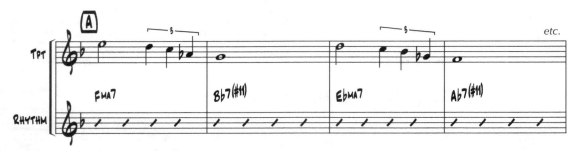

Example 14.10

Melodic Fragment

Thus far we have observed introduction examples in which a specific element is emphasized. For example, the "last section" technique provides a hint of the melody but disguises how the tune begins. The "vamp" technique offers a small glimpse of the harmonic flavor of the piece but without revealing the melody. Improvising over the chord changes provides the harmony, form, and style of the tune, but again omits the melody.

Another option is to use the beginning of the melody as an introductory device. This technique takes more thought and creativity, but it can be an effective way to introduce more than just the harmony and feel of the piece. Look for distinctive elements in the melody and take advantage of those elements as you construct the introduction.

This type of introduction is demonstrated in the next example using the piece "Why Not Now." In this case, a melodic fragment from the melody is scored for the entire ensemble in octaves and four-part harmony.

Example 14.11

The example shown above is reminiscent of example 14.6, the only other example in which the entire band enters at the beginning of the introduction. Both examples are the most exciting and dynamic of all the introductions shown thus far.

Unrelated Material

Composing an entirely new section for your introduction is always a possibility for any type or style of tune. This is obviously the most challenging option for the arranger but it has an added advantage: you can use that same material later in the chart, perhaps as an interlude or ending. You may want to emphasize an original chord progression rather than compose a new melody, but you can also add a new melody as well.

Harmony/Rhythm

This example illustrates a vamp that is not derived from the opening chord changes—this is new material. The harmony consists of an F pedal tone under suspended and altered dominants.

Example 14.12

Harmony/Rhythm + New Melody

The next example includes a melody over the harmonic/rhythmic foundation shown in the example seen immediately above. Notice that the melody enters the second time through, building intensity as the introduction is layered.

Example 14.13

The next example is the most ambitious introduction seen thus far. The Latin tune "Sabrosa" is the vehicle used for this interesting and exciting unrelated material. Here, "So What" voicings move through the keys of D minor and E♭ minor and the introduction concludes with a half cadence in G minor. Since "Sabrosa" begins with the ii of F major (Gmi7), this sets up the tune perfectly.

Example 14.14

An arrangement is in some ways comparable to a novel. The beginning of a novel may introduce the setting, tone, and characters of the story—and if done well, it will entice the reader to turn the page to see what happens next. A similar process occurs in music. If you write an introduction (and remember, not every arrangement needs one) the goal is to attract the listener's interest, compelling him or her to keep listening. Hopefully, as the arrangement unfolds, your work will cause the listener to think, "Oh, now I see how it all fits together."

Conclusion

The next chapter deals with the opposite end of the arrangement: the ending. Since the ending of an arrangement often uses material from the introduction, we will revisit many of the techniques from this chapter.

Chapter Summary

Common introduction types are:

1. Improvised introductions
2. Last section of the melody (often the last four bars)
3. Vamp (a repeating series of a few chords)
4. Melodic fragment used to construct introduction
5. Unrelated material (a completely new section)

Assignment 14.1

Introductions

Add an introduction to one of your already-existing four-horn arrangements.

Endings

Of all the elements required for a successful jazz arrangement, continuity is perhaps the most vital. Instead of just sewing together unrelated musical parts, arrangers should incorporate elements into their arrangements that create a sense of unity and connectedness. Endings and introductions play a role in this since they are often similar and constructed with the same material. In this chapter, some of the endings will resemble introductions from the last chapter and some won't. But they all share the same goal and purpose: to provide a natural-sounding way to conclude the chart. Introductions are important, obviously, because they are heard first by the listener. But endings are equally important—after all, you don't want a successful arrangement spoiled by an ending that does not fit the flavor and style of the work you've created. In planning the ending of your arrangement, you first need to decide whether or not a specific ending is even necessary. Often the piece can conclude with an ending as simple as a short note played by the entire group or perhaps a long held note with a fermata.

Jazz musicians have developed a repertoire of stock endings that have served the needs of performers for decades. Musicians learn these "tricks of the trade" by simply performing with a variety of other players. These stock endings can also be used by arrangers.

Stock Endings

A stock ending is a well-known ending that has, over a long period of time, become a common means by which to end a tune. These antiquated but effective endings are often performed on club date jobs. A thorough discussion of stock endings is beyond the scope of this book. However, four generalizations will help guide the discussion that follows:

1. On a swing tune, a band will often play a short concluding melody at the end of the tune. The two most common of these are:

   (a) The original ending of the Billy Strayhorn standard, "Take the A Train."
   (b) The so-called "Basie" ending which, although usually played by the pianist, may also be voiced for horns.

   These two endings are provided in the example below.

Example 15.1

2. On Latin tunes, the vamp placed at the end is usually the same material that was used for the introduction. A sustained tonic chord concludes the tune.
3. On a ballad, the tune will often end with a cadenza played by the primary melodic instrument. This cadenza is usually played over a sustained V chord leading to a sustained tonic chord.
4. Often the last four bars of a tune are repeated to form a tag ending.

Usually no discussion or planning is required to play these stock endings—jazz musicians know from experience when and how to use them. Arrangers also use these endings since they are such an integral part of the sound of jazz. So while jazz performers are able to fake these endings, arrangers can notate them in interesting and innovative ways. Therefore, we will integrate stock endings in our upcoming discussion.

Of course, there are many ways to end a chart that are more interesting and useful than a well-worn stock ending. The list below outlines some of the most common and useful endings used by arrangers. This is not meant to be a comprehensive list—instead, it is a resource to help you end your chart in a logical, musical way.

Common Ending Types

Endings can be categorized as follows:

- Tag
- Vamp borrowed from introduction
- Melodic fragment borrowed from introduction
- Unrelated material borrowed from introduction

This list reveals that the relationship between the introduction and the ending is a very close one indeed.

Style Considerations

Sometimes a given ending will work better in one style of tune than in another. The following chart indicates which endings are useful in each of the most common jazz styles. These are not hard and fast rules—just suggestions and observations of the way jazz musicians tend to do things.

Common Endings

Style	Types of Endings Common to That Style
Up-Tempo Swing	Tag ending Melodic fragment Unrelated material
Medium Swing	Tag ending Melodic fragment Unrelated material
Ballad	Tag Ritard to fermata (no specific ending inserted) Cadenza by the primary melody instrument
Latin	Vamp Tag ending Melodic fragment Unrelated material

Tags

The material that is repeated in a tag ending can vary according to the harmonic rhythm of the chord progression. In songs like "Take the A Train," "Satin Doll," and "All of Me," the last four bars would be a simple ii–V–I progression, like this:

Example 15.2

Tunes with a harmonic rhythm of one chord per measure could be "tagged" as follows:

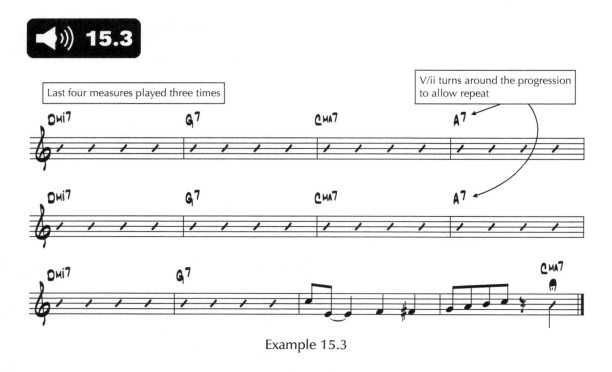

Example 15.3

This simple formula requires a secondary dominant, the A7, to "turn around" the progression (thus the name *turnaround*). The four-bar unit is played three times in this example. While three times is the norm, it sometimes is played only twice. Often a iii chord (an Emi7 in this case) substitutes for the I in the second statement of the progression. Also, the A7 usually contains chord tone substitutions such as a flatted ninth and flatted thirteenth, since it is functioning as the dominant of D minor (review the section on minor key progressions in chapter 6 if necessary). This tag can be used as a final improvised section and therefore repeated many times. An excellent example of this type of ending is Miles Davis' recording of "All of You" on the album *'Round About Midnight*. Notice also that I used the "Take the A Train" line depicted in example 15.1 to drive toward the fermata, though the "Basie" ending described above would have worked just as well.

A similar process occurs when the harmonic rhythm is twice as fast, as in tunes like

"Have You Met Miss Jones" and "Like Someone in Love." Here is what the last four bars of those tunes would look like:

Example 15.4

The third and fourth measures from the end are used for the tag in this case with the more rapid harmonic rhythm, and is illustrated below. The example concludes with the "Basie" ending.

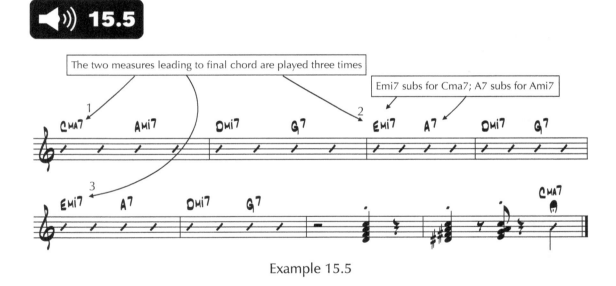

Example 15.5

Now that we have explored the manner in which jazz performers end tunes, it's time to discuss how arrangers go about the same process. While you should borrow some of the techniques from the "stock" ending library, you can also expand upon those approaches. Since you have the luxury of time and reflection, you can put more thought into it, tailoring those stock endings to fit what you have in mind.

In the following example, "Why Not Now" concludes with a tag ending. Instead of ending on a sustained tonic chord like the stock examples above, it ends on a short note. This example, in which the first two bars of the final four-bar section are used for the tag, is similar to example 15.5.

Example 15.6

In order to appreciate examples 15.6, 15.7, and 15.8, first listen to example 12.6 which is the four-horn combination version. Now, as you listen to example 15.6, you'll hear the brass countermelody drop out as the tag is repeated. The countermelody returns for the final statement. I felt that I could add some variety to the structure of the ending by layering the instruments.

The next two examples display a common ending technique involving modulation. In example 15.7, the first of the two, the middle statement of the tag is placed up a half step and the brass countermelody is again removed.

Example 15.7

Notice how much the tag is brightened by the brief modulation. Example 15.8 illustrates a tag in which the middle statement is moved up a minor third from the home key, taking the harmony even farther away.

Example 15.8

These examples demonstrate just how effective a tag ending can be. As the listener hears the characteristic repeat of the last section of the tune, there will be no doubt in his or her mind that the ending is on its way. For that reason, adding variety either through texture change (by omitting the brass) or harmonic variation (by putting the middle statement in another key) helps make this time-tested technique work even more effectively.

Vamp

As mentioned above, Latin tunes played on a club date gig often end with the same vamp that started the tune. This technique also works well for arrangers, as the following example of "Sabrosa" illustrates. This ii–V vamp was used as an introduction in chapter 14 (example 14.9). Take the time to revisit that example. For the ending, I added a melodic line to the vamp played by the horns, shown in the next example.

Example 15.9

Melodic Fragment

In chapter 14 (example 14.11) a fragment of the opening melody, scored for the entire band, was used as an introduction. This is an example of an exciting introduction that immediately grabs the listener's attention. Like the previous example in which an opening vamp was used for the ending, this melodic fragment also serves to unify the arrangement as an ending. This technique is illustrated below in the next example.

Example 15.10

Unrelated Material: Vamp

In chapter 14 (example 14.13) an introduction is provided for "Why Not Now" which utilizes a vamp. It is comprised of dominant suspended and altered chords and is paired with an unrelated melodic line played by the horns. This introductory material works well in other parts of the arrangement as a unifying element, and it is particularly effective for an ending. This is illustrated in the example shown below.

Example 15.11

Unrelated Material: Newly Composed Section

Using material composed especially for the introduction works well as an ending, as was illustrated in the vamp example above. Chapter 14 includes a rather elaborate introduction for "Sabrosa" in example 14.14. The following example revisits the first segment of that material—this time as an ending.

Example 15.12

Remember that not all arrangements require a specific ending. Use discretion as you decide on this important part of your project; it is the last thing the listener hears. But the point of an ending is to tie up the musical statement you've made. It's very important that the ending flows naturally and logically from the rest of the arrangement.

Chapter Summary

Ending Types:

1. Tag
2. Vamp borrowed from introduction
3. Melodic fragment borrowed from introduction
4. Unrelated material borrowed from introduction

Assignment 15.1

Endings

Add an ending to one of your already-existing four-horn arrangements.

Common Problems & Solutions

Jazz improvisers make mistakes. A solo may be satisfying to the listener but disappointing to the performer, or vice versa. Either way, a jazz musician performing live music cannot go back and repair whatever mistakes were made. The discipline of jazz improvisation is so demanding that the perfect solo is elusive if not impossible to achieve. Jazz arranging is equally demanding, but with one big difference: the arranger has time on his or her side. After all, reflection and deliberation are part of the process. That being said, in a task as challenging as jazz arranging, mistakes still do occur. Avoiding them is the purpose of this chapter.

While some errors are the result of sloppy work or incorrect application of jazz theory concepts, other problems arise out of good intentions. Often the arranger attempts certain effects that simply don't work. In this chapter, we will discuss some of the most common mistakes that arranging students make while at the same time offering suggestions on how to avoid these mistakes in the first place. The discussion below does not include obvious typographical errors such as missing accidentals, incorrect repeat signs, or transposition mistakes. The problems demonstrated below are harder to pin-point and are not so obvious. We will deal here with common mistakes that may look good on paper (or even sound good on a computer) but don't work when played by real musicians. This is a very important chapter because while the improviser performing live puts his mistake behind him immediately, the arranger's mistakes never go away.

Here are the most common mistakes I have seen throughout many years of teaching jazz arranging:

- Incorrect parallel harmonies
- Awkward lines, especially countermelodies
- Awkward repeated notes
- Overwriting
- Horns out of sync with the rhythm section

The following examples contain all of these common errors. By studying these examples, you can train yourself to avoid duplicating these mistakes in your own work. Hopefully, through experience, score study, and extensive listening, your arranging skills will mature and you will outgrow these types of errors.

In this chapter we will use the blues tune "Finding the Groove" as a vehicle for demonstrating these subtle yet important arranging mistakes. Example 16.1 contains the lead sheet for "Finding the Groove," and the harmonic analysis is in example 16.2. It would be useful to compare this blues tune to other blues tunes you may know. "Finding the Groove" has a very simple melody and is accompanied by resolving suspended chords. There are interesting rhythmic kicks in the last phrase that integrate melody and harmony with a series of substitute chords.

Example 16.1

ANALYSIS OF "FINDING THE GROOVE"

Example 16.2

In our previous discussion of form, I mentioned that blues melodies are usually played twice before the arrangement moves forward, usually into a solo section. Often the melody is played by a single horn (or unison horns) the first time with a thickened texture applied for the repetition of the melody. This is the case here; the melody is performed first by the trumpet and is joined by one or more horns as the melody is repeated. Only the second time through the melody is illustrated in the following examples. Most examples are written for trumpet, alto sax, and rhythm section. There is one example written for three horns (in which a trombone is added to the ensemble) and the final "correct" version is scored for four horns. Get ready to experience some bad writing!

Parallel Harmonies

Arranging students often write parallel harmony parts without any regard for their function. Ignoring the harmonic structure by simply adding a lower part that follows the melodic contour almost always leads to problems.

Parallel Thirds

Harmonizing the melody of "Finding the Groove" in thirds seems like it would be effective, but in the next example we see a serious problem: the harmonizing note is too unstable. Examine the two-horn version in example 16.3 and listen to the audio recording.

Example 16.3

In the initial six measures, the melody is harmonized a minor third below. Choosing a minor third as the harmonizing interval below the melody provides notes available in the key of C which would perhaps be a tempting choice for the arranger.

Problem: Unstable Harmonization

The whole notes in measures 1, 3 and 5 sound odd. Why? The harmonizing note (the A in measures 1 and 3 and the D in measure 5) is the thirteenth of each dominant chord. On dominant chords like these, the thirteenth needs to be supported by more fundamental chord tones under it. Try playing the horn parts on the piano while holding down the roots in your left hand. You'll find that the horn parts make the chord roots sound incorrect. Also, measure 6 contains a wrong note—the E natural is a major seventh above an F, and would therefore conflict with the seventh of the F7 chord. Although the harmonization in minor thirds provides very rich harmonic choices in the last four measures, they may be too colorful for the context of this tune. The lower note is the raised eleventh of each of the dominant chords as the progression moves around the circle of fifths. Try playing this on the piano, too—I think you'll hear that the raised elevenths also give the impression of instability.

Solution: Try Unison Instead

If there were more voices (i.e., horns), the chords could be scored in either four-way close or drop-2, which would give more support to the melody. Since there are only two horns in this example, however, that option is not available. Therefore, in a two-horn arrangement, the solution may be to eliminate harmony notes altogether. Recall that all of the examples in this chapter are based on the second statement of the melody. If you simply add the alto sax in unison with the trumpet, you'll be thickening the texture.

Incidentally, there is one positive aspect to this example that I will expand upon in the next chapter: the alto sax is integrated with the rhythm section in measure 7. This works well here, and we will see this again in each of the upcoming examples.

Parallel Fourths

The next example illustrates a harmonization in parallel fourths. Arranging students often use these more strident harmonic choices in the belief they will make their arrangements sound more modern and hip.

Example 16.4

Problem: Harmony In Fourths Too Strident

Parallel fourths in this setting are too "edgy" for the flavor of this piece as the recording makes very clear. Quartal harmony should be used with caution. As I pointed out in chapter 6, "Tertian Harmony," most of what we do is based on tertian harmonic principles. Using parallel fourths is more of an effect rather than a voicing method.

Solution: Try Unison or Guide Tone Harmony Instead

The solution suggested above is valid here as well. Unison would be the better choice. However, adding guide tones (thirds and/or sevenths) at certain locations helps to stabilize the harmony. For example, using an A in measure 6—perhaps resolving from a suspended tone Bb—would provide a harmonic foundation in the middle of the melody.

Awkward Lines

Writing melodic and tuneful harmony parts (and countermelodies) is one of our most daunting challenges as jazz arrangers, and example 16.5 illustrates a particularly awkward accompanying line in the alto sax.

Example 16.5

Problem: Awkward Lines In The Pick-Up Measure

In the example shown above, the attempt to emphasize the suspended tones of the C and F chords is a good idea and will be used in the "correct" version in example 16.11. But the opening accompaniment line G–Bb–F is too disjunct. As the figure is repeated, the problem is compounded. Take the time to play it on the piano or on your own instrument. The leap of the descending fourth feels and sounds odd. In addition to the full ensemble version shown above, I have also provided a recording that omits the trumpet part in order to expose the awkward alto sax line. Listen to them both carefully.

   (See example 16.5)

The Solution: Integrate the Alto Line with the Rhythm Section

Since the alto sax has the same rhythm as the rhythm section in measure 7, this concept could be expanded for the entire melody. The alto line could simply play the suspended tones (the F in the C7sus4 and the Bb in the F7sus4) and resolve them, which is what the piano part calls for. You could also try a G–Gb–F line in the pick-up notes in measure 2, and a C–B–Bb line in measure 4. This solution provides a better countermelody while still emphasizing the suspended fourths. Notice the last phrase is in unison—this works well here.

Awkward Repeated Notes

Repeated notes can be a problem if they are uncomfortable to play. This occurs most often in note values of eighth notes or shorter. "Upbeat to downbeat" repeated notes are normally not a problem to play comfortably, but "downbeat to upbeat" repeated notes are almost always awkward as we will see in the next example.

Example 16.7

The Problem: Repeated Notes

In "Finding the Groove," the C7sus4 and F7sus4 chords are sounded on the "and" of four in the first six measures. It might be tempting to harmonize the melody by putting the alto sax on the seventh of the chord, creating a major second dissonance with the melody note. Doing so, however, creates awkward repeated notes (two B flats in a row in the pickup measure and in measure 2, and two E flats in a row in measures 4 and 6). These repeated note figures would be difficult to swing and would feel unnatural to the performer. In addition to the full ensemble version shown above, I have also provided a recording that omits the trumpet part (see below).

   (See example 16.7)

Solution: Unison Trumpet and Alto

In chapter 11, "Two-Part Writing," example 11.14 demonstrates harmonizing with unusual intervals such as sevenths and seconds. While it worked very well in that case, it would be difficult to avoid the repeated notes in example 16.7 above. Also, harmonizing whole notes with dissonant intervals (as is the case here) tends to obscure the melody. Major seconds can be very effective with shorter note values, adding a "pop" to an important note at just the right time. The fact that this choice results in awkward repeated notes would suggest that you should avoid this option altogether and write the two horns in unison. Remember that writing in unison is not a "cop-out"—it's a wonderful way to create a whole new timbre by combining instruments. Also, harmonizing the root of a chord is inherently difficult with only two horns. This is why unison has been suggested several times throughout this chapter.

Overwriting

This next example highlights a very common problem for beginning arrangers: writing lines that are too busy or active.

Example 16.9

Problem: Too Much Complexity

Both performer and listener want the music to sound good—and *feel* good, too. Excessive complexity in any musical element (e.g., melody, harmony, rhythm, instrumentation) can detract from the enjoyment of the music. In the example seen above, the alto line is busy from the start and gets even more complicated as it progresses. It also covers up the melody in measure 2, violating the simple rule of "writing in the holes" of the melody. I have heard students justify this type of writing to me by saying, "It sounded good on the computer." While that may be true (from the student's perspective anyway), this line is too complex for this simple blues tune. This is one of the dangers of writing directly onto the computer rather than with pencil and paper. It would take quite an effort to write out this alto line by hand, yet on the computer it would take relatively little time. Writing with pencil and paper can contribute to simpler arrangements.

The Solution: Write "In The Holes" Of The Melody

The melody is all-important; obscuring it is almost never a good idea. Write your countermelody when the primary melody pauses. Composers have been doing that for centuries in all forms of music. The countermelody seen above, however, is too busy even when the melody pauses. Remember: strive to write with simplicity.

Lack of Integration with the Rhythm Section

This next example comes closer to an effective solution but still has a serious problem. This three-horn version contains a problem that is more common than you may think.

Example 16.10

Problem: Horns Not In Sync With Rhythm Section

In example 16.10, the alto sax and trombone add simple chord tones to the C and F suspended chords, with the trombone resolving the suspensions (F to E in measures 1 and 3 and B♭ to A in measure 5). Notice that the accompanying horns are integrated with the rhythm section in measures 7 and 8. These are all positive qualities of this example. The problem in this version occurs in the final three measures where the rhythmic kicks for the accompanying horns are not synchronized with the rhythm section. As you listen to this recording, you may be surprised that students actually make an error this glaring. Neglecting to integrate horns with the rhythm section actually occurs quite frequently.

Solution: Sync Horns with Rhythm Section

The alto sax and trombone parts must be written on the "and" of beat 4 in measure 8 and on the "and" of beats 2 and 4 in measures 9–10; in this example the horns are written incorrectly on beats 1 and 3.

The "Correct" Version

Finally, example 16.11 illustrates a version that works well. Notice that the alto sax doubles the trumpet melody in the first seven measures as was suggested in several of the solutions above. Also, observe that although the accompanying line in the lower horns is very simple, it highlights the resolution of the suspended tone in the C and F chords. The horns are correctly integrated with the rhythm section in measures 7 and 8, and the example ends with the sequential melody supported by four-way close harmonization with all four horns aligned properly with the rhythm section.

Example 16.11

Chapter Summary

1. Parallel harmonizations: accompanying parts must match the harmonic structure.
2. Awkward lines: use the rules outlined for writing effective countermelodies.
3. Repeated notes: avoid repeated eighth notes in most cases, particularly "downbeat to upbeat" eighth notes.
4. Overwriting: writing with simplicity is almost always preferable to complexity.
5. Lack of integration of horns and rhythm section: align the melodic element with the harmonic element, especially on anticipated figures like the "and" of four.

The Complete Arrangement

Throughout this book I have used the tunes "Why Not Now," "Sabrosa," and "December Serenade" to demonstrate various melodic treatments, introductions, and endings. An arranger could consider each of these tunes complete and ready to perform by simply choosing one of the texture options presented thus far, adding an introduction, an ending, and notating the chord changes in the horn parts for solos. However, much of the enjoyment of writing an arrangement comes from composing new sections which can really make a project your own unique creation. Also, learning how to add new material to the basic form of a tune is excellent training for any big band writing you may do in the future. This is a wonderful chance to gain experience doing some real composing.

This chapter will focus on the following sections:

- Solo backgrounds
- Soli section
- Interlude
- Shout chorus
- Send-off

345

In order to examine these additional sections, full transposed scores of "Why Not Now," "Sabrosa," "December Serenade," and "Finding the Groove" are presented in their entirety in this chapter. Each is written for trumpet, alto sax, tenor sax, trombone, piano, bass, and drums. These scores contain various labels and annotations that point out the arranging techniques being employed at a given spot. Also, the text that follows each example will further analyze the examples with a special emphasis given to the most recent additions.

You'll recognize many of the melodic treatments in these arrangements because they are derived from the methods described in chapter 12. There will also be introductions and endings that you've heard before. You may recall that all of the melodic treatments, introductions, and endings seemed to work quite well. For these final arrangements however, I chose the versions that I felt worked the best. But keep in mind that there is an infinite number of ways to arrange these tunes—that's what makes jazz arranging so enjoyable.

In chapter 3, I provided some schematic diagrams in order to demonstrate the various ways in which tunes in different forms can flow. As I arranged these example tunes, I used these diagrams to help provide a structure. As was pointed out in chapter 10, having a plan from the beginning will allow you to write with more continuity and unity. Therefore I have provided a formal sketch for each tune with much more detail than was included in the schematic diagrams in chapter 3.

Creating the Score and Parts

When producing the score and parts for a performance of your music, set the highest standards for yourself and give yourself ample time to meet those standards. There is nothing more frustrating as an arranger than hearing mistakes made by the musicians that are the result of sloppy work on your part. Think of it this way: when a band plays your chart, it should sound just the way you intended it to sound—with or without your presence. In order to help you avoid notation errors, I have listed some tried-and-true suggestions below. This list is not exhaustive, but if you follow this advice it will take you a long way toward removing obstacles—and letting your music speak for itself.

Notation Suggestions

- Try to avoid odd spellings (e.g., E♯, B♯) unless there is a really good reason to use them, such as a chromatic passage.
- Don't be afraid to use enharmonic spellings that don't match the prevailing key if using them makes the music easier to read.
- Use courtesy accidentals when appropriate (and you may need them more often than you think).
- Don't beam three eighth notes together if they are not a triplet.
- Don't beam eighth notes over rests.
- Don't beam notes across the middle of a measure.
- Articulations are meant to convey your stylistic intent exactly. This is particularly important in groups with more than one horn, as they must match stylistically. Pay close attention to quarter notes, as they are usually (but not always) played

short. If the chart is notated correctly, no discussion should be necessary among the players.

- Place articulations above the staff, not below.
- Tempo and style must be in both the score and the parts.
- Don't write an entire measure for pick-up notes.
- Indicate instrument changes (e.g., mute changes for brass or doubles for woodwinds) at the end of the phrase before the change occurs, and allow sufficient time to make the change.

Layout Suggestions

- Score and staff must be identical. A sample part of "Finding the Groove" is located in appendix B.
- Rehearsal letters normally occur every eight bars, or every twelve bars in a blues.
- Put double bars at each rehearsal letter and at the beginning of each first ending.
- Staff spacing, measure spacing, and note spacing should be consistent.
- Parts usually have four measures per line, although there are exceptions to this rule. First and second endings sometimes change this.
- Multimeasure rests are normally no more than eight measures to facilitate placement of rehearsal letters.
- Tape your parts accordion-style using masking tape.
- If you're writing by hand, use a ruler for all bar lines and stems.
- Begin each part with a dynamic marking.
- Play through every part on your own instrument—this may not reveal exactly what it will feel like for the specific instrument the part is written for, but it is a great way to find awkward lines, repeated notes, etc.
- Use standard written signs to communicate the road map to the band (e.g., repeat signs, the D.S., the D.C., the coda sign). Taking the time to give verbal road map directions to the band can eat up precious rehearsal time. However, if these signs result in a confusing road map, it may be wise to write out the repeated music.
- Eliminate unneeded staves: optimize staff systems (e.g., the bass clef staff of a piano part).
- Be aware of page turns in the parts. Put rests on the bottom of the page for this purpose.
- Finish your parts at least a day before distributing them so that you can thoroughly proofread them.

"Why Not Now"

If needed, refer back to the lead sheet and analysis in chapter 2 (although by now you've heard so many versions of this tune that the melody, harmony, and form should be very familiar). Before you examine the score and listen to the audio track, look over the diagram below. Notice that there is an introduction that also serves as both ending and interlude. The interlude is also used for the solo section, providing the soloists different material on which to improvise. This melodic treatment is identical to the combination texture described in chapter 12 (see example 12.6). Also, the introduction/ending is the "unrelated material: vamp" variety discussed in chapters 14 and 15.

"Why Not Now" Form Breakdown

Measure	Section of Form	Description
1	Introduction	First 8 bars; rhythm section on V pedal
9		Second 8 bars; add octave horn line
17	A	Unison saxes
25	A'	Add brass countermelody in octaves
33	B (Bridge)	Brass harmonized melody; saxes answering lines
41	A'	Same as previous A' (to coda last time)
49	Interlude (same as intro)	Solos: tenor, trumpet, piano
57	Unison horn line from intro	Unison horn line on tenor solo only, first chorus only
65	A	Solo continues
73	A'	Solo continues
81	B (Bridge)	Backgrounds last chorus of trumpet solo
89	A'	Solo continues
97	Interlude	Soli for all horns
105	A	Soli continues
113	A'	Soli continues
121	B (Bridge)	piano plays bridge melody
D.S. to 41	A'	
49	Interlude	To Coda after measure 56
Coda	Unison horn line	End on Bma7(b5)

Why Not Now

stark, colorless sus voicing, for effect
enesmble support in the drums

slash chord (D/F7 = F13♭9)

sus voicing with more color - includes 9th and 13th

Example 17.1

Score Layout

Before we discuss the details of the actual music, look carefully at the layout of the score. While it is beyond the scope of this book to discuss every aspect of notation and score layout, it will be beneficial to point out a few specifics. The score order is trumpet, alto sax, tenor sax, trombone, piano, bass, and drums. The horns are grouped together; notice that the bar lines pass through them and there is a bracket on the left side. The score is minimized occasionally to save space, most often by eliminating the bass clef of the piano part. Notice the score directions especially as they guide the musicians through the solo section. When inserting instructions in your score, it is important to be concise, yet clear and accurate. There is a lot to know about score and part layout—take the time to study this important subject along with the topic of arranging.

The Arrangement

In this treatment of "Why Not Now," a recurring interlude brings unity to the arrangement. This same interlude serves as the introduction, ending, and background figures. Juxtaposing dissonant harmonies in a traditional bebop setting can be very effective—both enjoyable to listen to and especially fun to improvise over.

As mentioned above, I chose the combination texture for the melody. I added the simple ascending scale figure in measures 40 and 128, first seen in the two-horn versions in chapter 11. This line serves as connective tissue between sections. The introduction/ending is the "unrelated vamp" type. While you will recognize some of this arrangement from previous examples, there are five sections that will be discussed below in more detail:

- Solo backgrounds
- Interlude
- Soli
- Ending
- Send off

As you read the following you will need to refer back to the full score, especially to the horn reductions that are included at various points.

Solo Backgrounds

Adding background lines to the solo section gives the soloist a more exciting and intense setting in which to improvise. An arranger must take care to write these accompanying lines in a manner that adds to the excitement of the solo section but does not interfere with the soloists. Simple "guide tone" lines work well, as well as blues scale melodies that add to the intensity of the solo section. Take care when choosing the rhythms for your background figures—keep them simple! Half notes and whole notes (along with an occasional syncopated figure) keep the lines where they belong—in the background. Example 17.2 illustrates background lines for "Why Not Now," placed in the bridge of the form. They are extremely simple for two reasons. First, they are in unison. This makes them very flexible in case you want to have an open section for improvised solos. The unison background parts, which are in every part, are played on cue. Second, they follow the sequential pattern of the harmony. Each statement begins on the third of the ii chord in each progression, culminating in an extended version in the third statement.

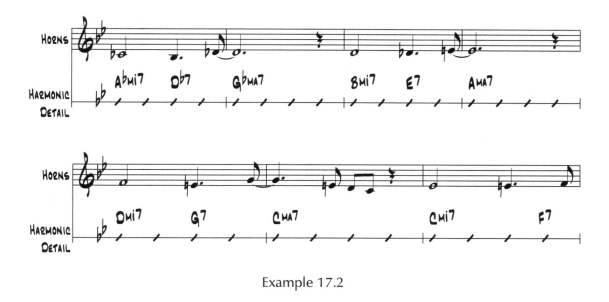

Example 17.2

Interlude

An interlude is a section of new or related material added to the form of the piece that serves to bridge sections together. It can connect the first complete melodic statement with the solo section—the place where the soloist can begin to improvise. The simplest method of creating an interlude is to recycle the introduction as the interlude. This unifies the arrangement. "Why Not Now" utilizes the introduction as an interlude to begin the solo (measure 49) and soli sections (measure 97), as well as for the ending.

Soli

A soli is a written group solo. It normally is scored in either unison or in a homophonic texture, but it can also contain several overlapping lines. It is often located after the solo section and frequently follows a rhythm section soloist. This gives the horn players the rest needed to play what may be a technically demanding passage. It is often the length of only one or two sections of the form, or it could be composed over the entire form. Its melodic material often comes from a transcribed solo. Some of the best examples of this type of writing are from the group Supersax, whose repertoire included transcribed Charlie Parker solos arranged for five saxophones.

The AABA model (described in chapter 3) suggests that soli or "shout" sections often last for only the first two A sections. This is the technique used here. The soli in "Why Not Now" follows the piano solo. It begins with the interlude at measure 97 using syncopated suspended chords voiced with the root on top. Two A sections make up the remainder of the soli. The next example offers a comparison between the original A section melody and the melody written for the soli. Pay close attention to the rhythm of the lines; they are most similar at the end of each eight-bar phrase. An effective way to provide continuity is to tie sections together using similar rhythmic shapes.

Example 17.3

My conception of the soli in "Why Not Now" involves rhythmic intensity in the interlude. This is then followed by more lyrical melodic lines (in the A sections) that are rhythmically related to the original melody. I have treated the A sections with a blend of unison, octave, and homophonic writing.

Interlude Within the Soli (Measures 97–104)

The horn reduction from the score is reprinted below with more detail in example 17.4. Note the stark voicing of the suspended chord in measures 97–98. It is constructed of (from the top-down) the root, fifth, fourth, and root. Suspended chords often include the ninth and sometimes the thirteenth—but these tones are omitted here, providing more power to the voicing. Measures 99–100 include a good example of a slash chord (D over F7) resulting in an F13(♭9) chord. A more colorful suspended chord voicing is placed in measures 101–102, which works to decrease the tension as the soli drives toward the more harmonically traditional A sections. Finally, notice the secondary dominant approach to the F7(♯9)(♭13) in measure 103.

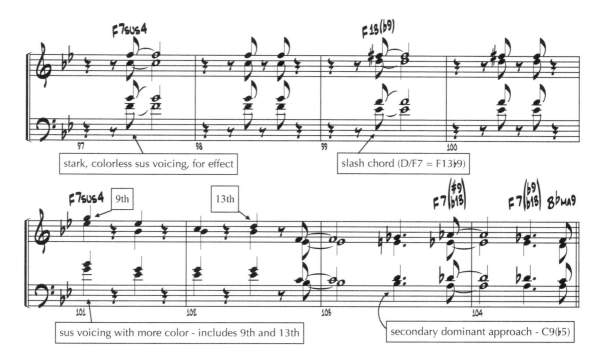

Example 17.4

First A Section Within the Soli (Measures 105–112)

The first four bars of this section are in four-part harmony. The melody is constructed of a two-note sequence that becomes progressively more rhythmically syncopated. The voicings are in four-way close with diatonic approaches used in measure 108. The second four bars, written in unison, are reminiscent of the melody, especially the last phrase.

Second A Section Within the Soli (Measures 113–120)

I recall writing this section backward, first thinking about how it would end. This is generally a good idea because it encourages continuity in your writing. A novelist should probably know how a book will end in order for the plot to lead there—the same can be said for composers and arrangers. Therefore, to provide stability to the arrangement, the soli ends with the same material as the concluding scale passage found in the "Why Not Now" melody. This section begins in measure 113 with a rhythmic figure supported by the drummer.

While solis are much more common in big band writing, they can be a wonderful addition to small group arrangements. Composing a soli provides the opportunity for you to actually *compose* rather than just *arrange*.

The bridge follows the soli and is scored only for the rhythm section with the pianist playing the melody. This instrumentation choice cools down the arrangement and gives the horns a needed break before playing the last A section of the form leading to the ending in the coda.

Ending

After the bridge is stated by the pianist, there is a D.S. to the last A section of the melody in measure 41. After a jump to the coda, the arrangement ends with an abbreviated version of the introduction/interlude concluding with a sustained Bmaj7(b5) chord. The arrangement, therefore, adheres to the form suggested for AABA tunes in chapter 3. Ending with just the BA part of the form is very effective, rather than restating the entire form as the arrangement concludes.

Send-Off

A send-off is a brief musical thought placed at the beginning of the solo section which is voiced in all horns except the soloing instrument. I didn't use one in the final completed version of "Why Not Now" because I preferred the intensity of a solo section that begins with the interlude. Therefore, an additional example has been provided demonstrating this technique. Send-offs often last for four measures, after which the soloist begins to improvise. Send-offs usually have an infectious rhythm. They can also be repeated at the beginning of the next formal section, as is the case in example 17.5 below. The example is notated in concert pitch.

Example 17.5

"Sabrosa"

The next piece we will examine as a full arrangement is the Latin tune "Sabrosa." Again, there are sections you've heard before. There are two important sections we will be looking at: the three-horn background parts during the alto sax solo, and also the shout chorus. The formal diagram below illustrates the flow of the arrangement.

"Sabrosa" Form Breakdown

Measure	Section of Form	Description
1	Introduction	Piano solo, 8 bars; add bass and drums, 10 bars
19	A	Trumpet and alto in unison
35	A'	Add lower horns on countermelody; end section in 4 part harmony
51	B (Bridge)	Alto on bridge melody; section ends in 4 part harmony
67	A'	4 part harmony with contrasting 2 voice section. Conclude in 4 parts
83	Interlude	Same as intro; 8 bars of rhythm section, add horns voiced in 4 parts
101	A	Alto sax solo with slightly altered chord changes
117	A'	Alto solo continues; backgrounds in other horns
133	B (Bridge)	Alto solo continues
149	A'	Backgrounds return; leads to shout chorus
165	Repeating circle progression	Shout chorus; strong cadence in D minor
19	AA'BA'	head
Coda	Abbreviated intro material	Four bars; end on A♭sus

Sabrosa

378   ARRANGING FOR THE SMALL JAZZ ENSEMBLE

drop two voicings; alto omitted from first statement while finishing solo

Example 17.6

Score Layout

"Sabrosa" has a sixty-four bar form which presented a challenge for me as far as score layout is concerned. Fortunately, I was able to reduce the score in several locations. Notice that the arrangement begins with only a piano part in grand staff. Bass and drums are added for the second system and then the two melody instruments. Because this score was produced in Finale with optimized staff systems, all the parts are not displayed until the second page. The directions for the solo section are simple since the alto sax is specified as the only soloist. Also, the solo only lasts for one chorus, so the solo backgrounds are played as written (no need to write in the indication "play backgrounds on cue").

The Arrangement

This version of "Sabrosa" is similar to "Why Not Now" in the use of the interlude, as it is constructed of borrowed material from the introduction. However, the interlude is not used as a solo device in this piece. Also, while "Why Not Now" concludes with only the second half of the melody following the soli, "Sabrosa" states the melody (and the introduction) in its entirety. You'll also notice that this is an alto sax feature. The bridge is played by only the alto sax, and the only solo is for the alto player. The combination texture is used, as was illustrated in chapter 12 (example 12.9).

The solo section contains an interesting alteration from the original tune: it features a chord progression simplified from those found in the A sections of the melody. By replacing an unusual chord progression with something more conventional (in this case, simple ii–V progressions moving chromatically) you add something new to the arrangement while also providing a better solo vehicle for the musicians. There are two additional aspects of this chart that will be discussed in detail:

- Solo backgrounds are in three-part harmony
- Shout chorus

Solo Backgrounds

The backgrounds composed for the alto sax solo are a little more complicated and plentiful than what was scored in "Why Not Now," although the soloist still has plenty of room to play with only the rhythm section. They enter at measure 117, and offer a good example of writing for three rather than four horns.

Example 17.7

The challenge of writing for three horns is evident in this passage. These back-grounds highlight the compromise required as four-part chords are scored for three horns. The first chord in example 17.7 is voiced with the ninth on top, and the fifth is omitted from the structure. Each line moves naturally to the C7 chord tones: A moving to G and F moving to E. The following chord, the B13(b5), includes richer chord tones (the b9, 13, and 3) which lead to a quartal stack over the E7(♯9)(b13) (from the top down, C, G, and D). There is no third in this chord, but the strong voice leading from the previous structure leads the ear through the progression. The last two bars of example 17.7 include a more conventional treatment of three-voice writing where the third and seventh are included in each chord. The last two chords in particular omit the ninth from the harmony, which works well, but results in a less colorful voicing.

The most active lines occur as we get closer to the bridge and shout choruses. Example 17.8 illustrates the background lines that lead to the bridge.

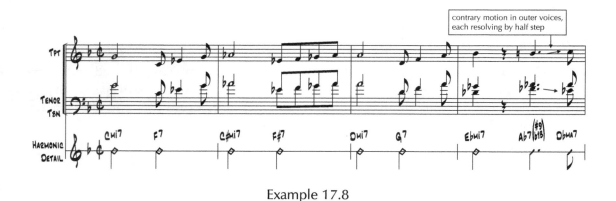

Example 17.8

The background parts are in unison as we approach the bridge, but the passage ends in three-part harmony. The contrary motion leading to the Dbma7 (the first chord of the bridge and the last measure of the example) works well in the outer voices. Contrast this material that drives toward the bridge with similar material leading to the shout chorus, illustrated below in example 17.9. Both sections begin in unison. The material in example 17.9 moves into harmony sooner, however, and offers an excellent example of open voicings beginning with the Emi7. Recall that one of the primary reasons to use open voicings is range. As the melody line (played by the trumpet) ascends, the trombone part is scored with the dropped second voice, making it much more playable.

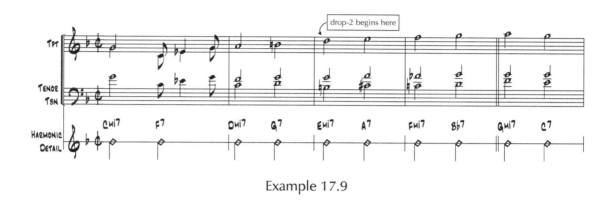

Example 17.9

Three-part writing takes more time and deliberation, as was emphasized in chapter 13. Listen to (and transcribe, if possible) some recordings of Art Blakey and the Jazz Messengers. These recordings are great examples of three-horn writing.

Shout Chorus

A shout chorus is the high point of an arrangement. It normally occurs after the solos have been played and before the return of the melody, normally about two thirds of the way through the arrangement. It can be constructed of new material, but is probably more often based on the melody. The shout chorus is an exciting event with horns usually voiced in harmony and with the drummer really driving the band. The shout chorus from "Sabrosa," based on a melodic fragment, is voiced initially in drop-2. This continues the voicing types used in the last background figure illustrated in example 17.9. Notice the difference in the effect created by the shout chorus in "Sabrosa" depicted below in example 17.10 as compared with the soli section in "Why Not Now" seen in example 17.3. This shout section is more aggressive and exciting—the horns are scored higher, and it features the drummer more prominently. From a harmonic standpoint it is based on a simple cadence figure in D minor which is stated four times.

Example 17.10

The voicings in example 17.10 provide a good example of the movement from open to close voicings as the melody descends on beat 3 to the "and" of 4 in the second measure of the example. Notice also the "So What" voicing in the second measure of the example. Recall that this is normally a five-voice structure, and there would normally be a B♭ on the bottom of this chord. The listener does not miss this note, however, because it is the root and is present in the bass part.

"December Serenade"

The ballad example, "December Serenade," is by far the simplest arrangement. It generally follows the form diagram for ballads in ABAC form laid out in chapter 3.

"December Serenade" Form Breakdown

Measure	Section of Form	Description
1	Introduction	Rubato piano solo, then pianist sets up time
9	A	Trumpet melody
17	B	Four part harmony
25	A'	Trumpet and alto on unison melody; tenor and trombone on unison countermelody
33	C	Brief blues line in octaves
49	ABA'C	Solos
9	ABA'C	Melody as before; end on held last note

December Serenade

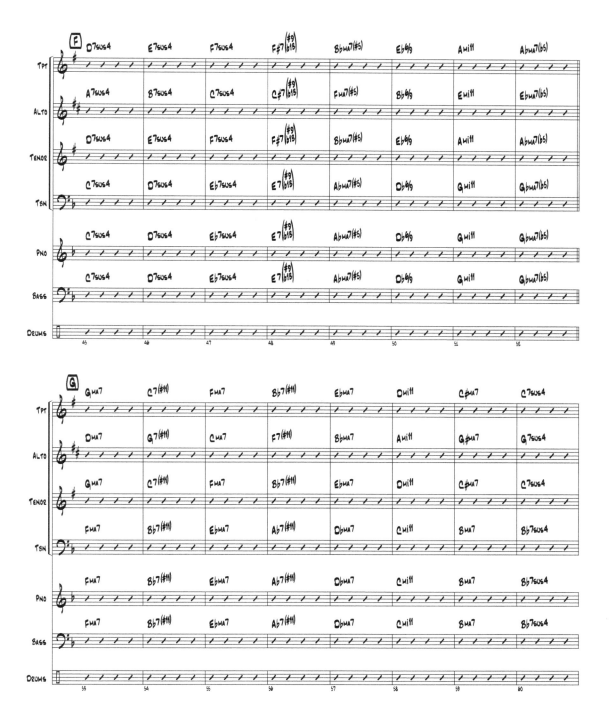

Example 17.11

Score Layout

The primary difference between this score and the other example tunes is that this chart has a separate section with just the solo changes. Since there are no other sections added to this piece (except the introduction), there is no need for a solo section integrated into the score. An alternative would be to notate the chord symbols for all the parts throughout the arrangement. I chose not to do that because I didn't want to clutter the score.

The Arrangement

"December Serenade" is the simplest of the four arrangements. For this complete version I chose the combination texture as depicted in chapter 12 (example 12.12). There have been no additional parts added because the melody, along with the improvisations over the rich harmonies, provides all the momentum that is needed for a successful performance. You should strive to avoid overwriting a piece like this.

"Finding the Groove"

In chapter 16 I used the blues tune "Finding the Groove" to illustrate problems and solutions. Therefore, we haven't seen various options of textures, introductions, and endings. As with the other example tunes, I chose a combination texture for the treatment of the melody. Integration of the horns and rhythm section occurs at two locations: in the introduction and in the second statement of the blues melody. I like to combine horns with the rhythm section; it adds an interesting color to the traditional rhythm section instruments.

"Finding the Groove" Form Breakdown

Measure	Section of Form	Description
1	Introduction	Rhythm section vamp
5		Add horns to vamp
13	Melody	Trumpet and alto
25	Melody	Add tenor and trombone countermelody
37	Blues changes	Solos: backgrounds last chorus of each solo
49		Bass solo
61		Dissonant-sounding backgrounds in horns
73		Shout chorus; end with tagged version of last melodic phrase around cycle of fifths
89	Introductory material	Rhythm section vamp
93		Add horns to vamp; end on C7($\sharp$11)

FINDING THE GROOVE

tonal cluster, with minor second dissonance between tenor sax
(playing the 5th of the chord) and trombone (playing the ♯11)

F chord less dissonant, with
minor third now separating lower voices;
♯11 remains on the bottom, moving to
sus 4 (B♭), then to third (A)

suspension resolves in trombone (the dropped voice)

tag ending, around circle of fifths

Example 17.12

Score Layout

This arrangement is very easy to follow because it reads down from start to finish with no D.S., D.C., or coda signs to worry about. There is a repeat sign for the solo section. The solo section also includes the direction "open for solos; BG (backgrounds) on cue." Unlike "December Serenade," I decided to notate the chord symbols for the entire horn section during the solo section since it is such a short form—only twelve bars. Notice also that the background parts are written for everyone so that any group of horns can play them at any time. This is why writing backgrounds in unison or octaves can make a performance very flexible.

The Arrangement

The arrangement of "Finding the Groove" is simple in just about every possible way. A basic vamp serves as the introduction and ending, and the melody is voiced in unison for the trumpet and alto sax. The lower horns add a simple and understated counter-melody at letter B. Note that this countermelody adheres to the suggestions made earlier in the text. It does not overwhelm the main theme—instead it "fills in the holes" in the melody and it joins the melody at the end of the phrase. This countermelody, scored for the tenor sax and trombone, includes an additional feature mentioned above—it is integrated with the rhythm section. Beginning in measure 31 these lower horns join the rhythm section's syncopated figures. Often, jazz ensembles present the appearance of two separate groups of musicians—wind players and rhythm section players. Combining horns with the rhythm section in various locations helps to unify the ensemble.

The arrangement of "Finding the Groove" includes two interesting sections that will be emphasized below:

- Background parts
- Shout chorus

Solo Backgrounds

The background lines are in unison and can be played by any horn combination at any time. It is a simple blues question and answer figure with a quote from the melody in the last four bars.

Example 17.13

Following the horn solos, a bass solo is scored as a contrasting two-chorus section. The horns enter in the second chorus with a dissonant version of the melody. The inner voice motion is highlighted in the horn reduction (measures 61–66). Notice that as the shout chorus approaches the harmonization becomes less dissonant.

Shout Chorus

The shout chorus of "Finding the Groove," illustrated in example 17.14, is the type of shout chorus that is based on the melody. This exciting moment of the chart is scored with the fifth of the C7 as the top note (the original chord is suspended quality; the C7 is a stronger harmonic choice). The reason for the choice of the G in the trumpet rather than simply rewriting the actual melody an octave higher has to do with the ensemble we're writing for here. A high concert C would work well in a big band setting, but in a small group setting it would be too high. In the example below, compare the original melody with the shout melody, particularly the rhythms. In the fifth measure of the example the pickup figure begins on beat 3, which is a refreshing and exciting change from the syncopated melody. Take note also of the voicing types utilized and the nonharmonic approaches.

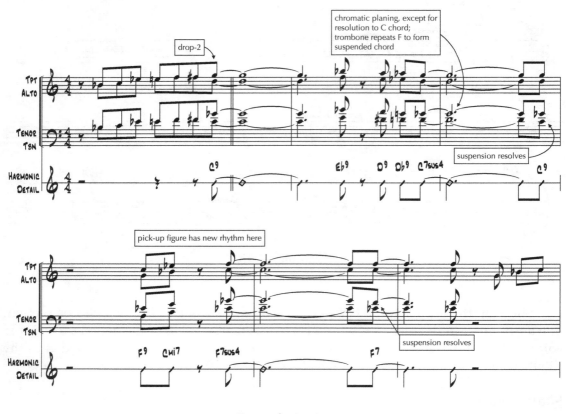

Example 17.14

Finally, because of the theme-based shout chorus, the arrangement does not restate the actual melody with a D.S. Instead, the arrangement concludes with a tagged ending, repeating the last phrase three times. Notice, however, that the pianist plays the middle statement as a solo (measures 82–83), and the harmony moves around the circle of fifths. The home key is reestablished when the horns return (measure 84–86).

The ending, as with "Why Not Now" and "Sabrosa," is a restatement of the introduction, tying the arrangement together.

Chapter Summary

These four arrangements include all of the elements that form successful jazz arrangements: melodies that are presented clearly, accompanying lines that compliment but do not overwhelm, background figures that energize the soloists, a variety of ensemble sections, and introductions and endings that unify the arrangement. It is my hope that these arrangements provide a musical summary of the concepts we have studied throughout the book.

Assignment 17.1

The Complete Arrangement

Complete a full arrangement for three or four horns and rhythm section. Arrange either a tune of your choice or one of the exercise tunes. In your arrangement, include the following elements:

- Introduction
- Melody
- Solo section, with backgrounds
- Soli or shout section
- A complete restatement of the melody or perhaps only half the form
- Ending
- Also could include an interlude or send-off before solo section

Conclusion

At various points along the way, I have made comparisons between jazz performers and arrangers. I did that because many of us are players first and arrangers second. While this is not true for everyone, most of us have attempted to master an instrument to some degree and we understand the triumphs and frustrations of that endeavor. The journey toward becoming a successful arranger or composer is much the same. You may remember a time when you were playing effortlessly—when the music was literally flowing out of you. Those treasured moments can also happen to arrangers. But for both performers and arrangers, these moments can only happen when the fundamentals are in place. Playing a great solo over a chord progression in the key of E♭ will be difficult if an E♭ scale, as well as a vocabulary of jazz patterns, is not second nature. Similarly, the construction of voicings and approaches, the acoustic properties of instrument families, the understanding of form and function—these "arrows" must be in the arranger's quiver before creativity can flow. Working through this book and the exercises has hopefully added to your working knowledge of the arranging process so that you can start developing your own voice as an arranger.

But this textbook is just the beginning. You must not neglect to listen continuously to jazz arrangements of all kinds. As you listen, pay close attention to what you're

405

hearing, and to what works and what does not. Take that knowledge to your sketchpad and borrow from the great minds that have formed this inspired music.

Jazz music is a big tent—there are many styles and trends within the jazz idiom. Fortunately what you've learned here can be applied to all types of music. In fact, you may one day find yourself using the techniques in this book to write in other genres such as pop, funk, or even country. If that is the case, remember this famous saying about musical style: "There are only two kinds of music: good and bad."

Be aware that your first attempts at writing may not be as successful as you would like. This is inevitable. The only way to improve is to keep writing. Success follows hard work. The most difficult aspect of this process is writing arrangements that are unified works and not individual sections that lack relationships. This takes a great amount of trial and error. But remember that the arranger has time to think things through, unlike the improviser who is creating music in the moment. While having the luxury of time is certainly helpful, it can also lead to "paralysis by analysis." Use your knowledge, but don't forget to be creative and natural.

In the competitive world of the music business, the all-around musician is the one who will succeed. Talent is important and wonderful to have in abundance—but the hard worker who can perform, compose, arrange, and is comfortable with technology will be the most prepared for a career in jazz. Having some business sense does not hurt either.

I hope you're able to use what you have learned here for your own ensembles (or in the case of educators, for your students). There is nothing more gratifying than hearing your own music performed by others and realizing that you've contributed a great chart to the jazz repertoire. Good luck as you explore this exciting field.

Appendices

Appendixes

Exercise Tunes

I composed three tunes especially for this book that are intended to be used as exercises. They are typical of most jazz standards. The three most common feels are represented here: swing, Latin, and ballad. Two forms are represented: AABA and ABAC.

ABAC Swing Exercise Tune

This medium swing tune in F minor is enjoyable to play (and to arrange) because of the contrasting rhythms among the sections. The A and C section melody is simple and would work well harmonized with diminished seventh approaches as the melody ascends in the first three measures. The tune moves between two keys in the A and C sections: F minor and Db major. There is also ample room for a countermelody to be inserted during melodic long tones. The B section consists of chromatically descending ii–Vs with a very active melody. Try not to overwrite a section like this. Section D is similar to section B, but has a slower harmonic rhythm.

This tune was used in chapter 11 to demonstrate instrumental blend and contrast. Please refer to those audio tracks to hear a recording of this tune.

ABAC Swing Exercise Tune

AABA Latin Exercise Tune

This Latin tune is in a bossa nova feel and begins in G minor. The melody has a blues flavor, especially the pick-up notes. The A, B, and D sections contain long held tones where a countermelody could fit nicely. There are some prominent raised eleventh chords that provide a brightness to the tune. The bridge (letter C on the lead sheet) consists of a "call and response" pattern between the rhythm section (the suspended chords) and the melody, which moves sequentially. Incorporating one or more horns into the rhythm section could be effective here.

AABA Ballad Exercise Tune

This pretty tune represents the jazz ballad repertoire with a sequential A section melody and a faster-paced bridge. The A section of this tune explores the keys of Eb and G minor. The bridge is comprised of ii–V–I progressions in F major, Gb major, Bb major, and Eb major. Again, take advantage of the long tones in the melody as opportunities to insert melodic motion in other voices.

AABA BALLAD EXERCISE TUNE

Sample Part

Creating clear, concise, and accurate parts for your musicians to read is critical to the success of your arrangements. Examine the sample part from "Finding the Groove" on the following page. This is the first page of the trumpet part. Take note of the comments regarding the tempo marking, solo section, articulations, rehearsal letters, and double bars. Naturally, this part matches the score exactly.

Finding the Groove

Trumpet

Robert Larson

Staff Paper

Several varieties of staff paper may be downloaded from the website that accompanies this book, www.SmallJazzEnsemble.com. However, for your convenience, the same staff paper has been provided here. Feel free to make copies of the staff paper provided below. The staff paper has been positioned slightly to the right of center, away from the spine of the book, to make it easier to make copies of these pages. The following kinds of staff paper are provided:

- Plain staff paper for general use
- Three-staff sketch paper (portrait orientation)
- Three-staff sketch paper (landscape orientation)
- Score paper for two horns and rhythm
- Score paper for three horns and rhythm
- Score paper for four horns and rhythm

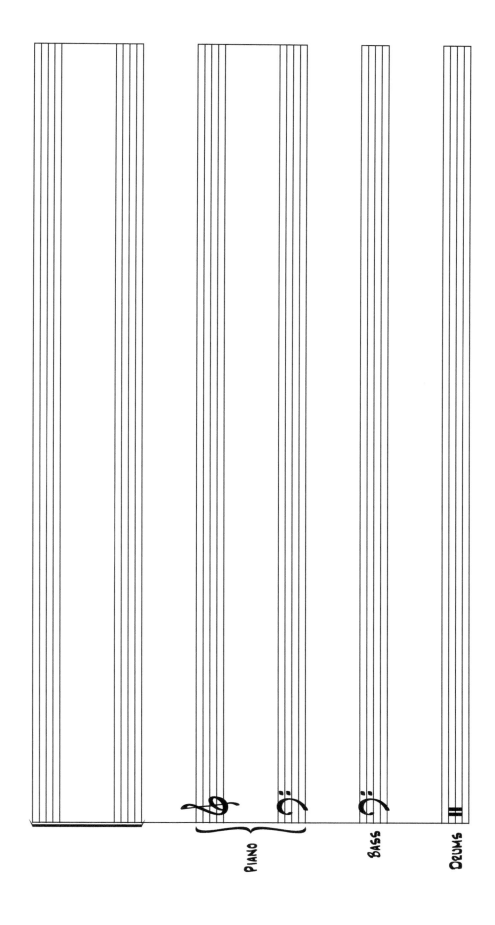

Index

AABA form, 6, 30, 31
ABAC form, 6, 31, 32
altissimo register, 51
alto saxophone, 49
approach, 149
articulation markings, 45
awkward lines, 333
awkward repeated notes, 335

background figures, 62
ballad, 20, 31, 32
baritone saxophone, 50
bass, 61
blend, 44, 201
blues, 7, 32
bucket mute, 49

chord over chord, 139
chord positions, 79
chord tone substitutions, 78
chromatic parallel approach, 153, 155, 156
chromatic planing, 153
circle of fifths, 82, 103
close voicing, 76
cluster voicing, 283, 285
comping, 58, 59
countermelody, 203
counterpoint, 204
cup mute, 47, 49

diatonic approach, 149, 155
diatonic planing, 149
diminished seventh approach, 149, 150, 155, 157
dominant approach, 149, 151, 156
dominant quartal structures, 128
double neighboring tones, 147, 152

drop-2 voicing, 115, 116
drop-2/4 voicing, 117
drop-3 voicing, 117
drum notation, 62
drum set, 61

enclosures, 147
endings, 307

four-way close, 76

guide tones, 204, 206
guitar, 61

Harmon mute, 47
homophony, 28

ii–V vamp, 296
ii–V–I progression, 104, 116
interlude, 361
introduction, 289
inversions, 79

lack of integration with rhythm section, 339
last section of melody as introduction, 292
layout suggestions, 347

melodic fragment as ending, 317
melodic fragment as introduction, 298
modal interchange, 17, 21
mute, 47, 49

neighboring tones, 147, 152
nonchromatic parallel approach, 153
nonharmonic tones, 147
notation suggestions, 346

open voicing, 76, 115

overwriting, 337

parallel approach, 149, 153, 158
parallel fourths, 331
parallel harmonies, 329
parallel thirds, 329
passing tones, 147
pedal tones, 48
piano, 60
polychord, 139
polyphony, 28

quartal harmony, 125, 283, 285
quartal voicing, 126, 127
quartet, 198
quintet, 201

rhythm changes, 12
rhythm section, 57
rhythmic notation, 59, 62, 63

saxophone, 49
saxophone ranges, 51
send-off, 364
septet, 202
sextet, 202
shell voicing, 81, 282
shout chorus, 383, 401
slash chord, 137, 138, 282
slash notation, 58, 59, 62
"So What" voicing, 129
soli, 361
solo backgrounds, 360, 381, 400
song forms, 5
stock arrangements, 29
stock ending, 308
stop time, 293
straight mute, 47, 49
suspended chords, 139

tag ending, 308, 309
tenor saxophone, 50
tertian harmony, 75
texture, 28
three-part writing, 281
triad, 75, 282
tritone substitution, 21
trombone, 47
trombone slide positions, 48

trumpet, 45
trumpet range, 46
turnaround, 310
two-bar repeat, 62
two-part writing, 202

unison, 28
upper extensions, 76

vamp, 295, 315, 318
voice leading, 80
voicing, 73

CPSIA information can be obtained
at www.ICGtesting.com
Printed in the USA
BVHW021613090223
658205BV00007B/626